Discover True North

A 4-Week Approach to Ignite Your Passion and Activate Your Potential

Anne Bruce

McGRAW-HILL

New York Chicago San Francisco Lisbon
London Madrid Mexico City Milan New Delhi
San Juan Seoul Singapore Sydney Toronto

2 3 4 5 6 7 8 9 0   DSH/DSH   0 1 0 9

ISBN 0-07-140300-0

McGraw-Hill books are available at special quantity discounts to use as premiums and sales promotions, or for use in corporate training programs. For more information, please write to the Director of Special Sales, Professional Publishing, McGraw-Hill, Two Penn Plaza, New York, NY 10121-2298. Or contact your local bookstore.

This book is printed on acid-free paper.

Library of Congress Cataloging-in-Publication Data

Bruce, Anne, 1952–
    Discover true north : a 4-week approach to ignite your passion and activate your potential / Anne Bruce.—1st ed.
        p. cm.
Includes bibliographical references and index.
    ISBN 0-07-140300-0 (pbk. : alk. paper)
    1. Self-actualization (Psychology) 2. Success—Psychological aspects. I. Title.
    BF637.S4B82 2003
    158.1—dc21
                                2003011272

This book is dedicated to the courageous and beautiful children of St. Jude Children's Research Hospital and to their extraordinary doctors, nurses, staff, and volunteers. Your devotion and commitment to a higher purpose remains a steady compass from which all of us can derive inner guidance and witness firsthand the power of the collective spirit of humanity. I also dedicate this book to St. Jude's founder, Danny Thomas, a man who exemplified the meaning of following True North when he vowed in a prayer to St. Jude Thaddeus, "Show me my way in life, and I will build you a shrine." And he did.

Contents

Foreword

When we think about some of the choices we've made in the past, how often do we find ourselves saying, "I knew I should have listened to myself. I could have saved myself a lot of time, energy, and heartache"? But too often we didn't listen to that inner voice. This voice is often called the unconscious wisdom, intuition and instinct, higher self, or greater spirit. Anne Bruce—author, professional speaker, and workshop facilitator—has a different, more evocative term: "True North." Just as the North Star guided sailors in times past, our personal True North offers a grounding point of reference, a steady hand to navigate life's often rocky course. It leads us to a place where we are our authentic selves, and life is simpler because we aren't trying to *look good* or to *please others*.

In today's fast-changing, complex environment, we have seen how, especially in corporate America, we can become derailed, consumed with ego, and internally alienated from our higher self and purpose. Caught up in the fast pace of life, we don't take the necessary time to pause and reflect, and to ask ourselves, "What am I doing? Where am I going?" And now more than ever, as our world becomes more visibly entwined and interconnected, we need to reassess who we are and where we stand. And this starts on an individual basis.

Anne Bruce, both graciously and passionately, invites you to connect, or perhaps reconnect, with this deeper way of knowing. Drawing from hundreds of workshops she has run, she has distilled her experience into a series of provocative self-assessments, questions, and exercises. She guides us to listen, trust, and act from our True North. She shows us how to not be a victim, but rather to be the author of our life story. Imagine a world in which people are guided by True North to their authentic self—deeply connected to themselves, to their calling, and to others. What a different world it would be.

Birute Regine
Coauthor of *The Soul at Work*
Cambridge, Massachusetts
Autumn 2003

Preface

This is a book about transformation—the nuts-and-bolts, optimistic, and practical transformation not only of ourselves, but of our world. It's a personal invitation, from me to you, to play a significant role in this process, both at home and at work, over the next 4 weeks.

Maybe you are someone who is seeking greater personal growth and happiness. You may be asking questions like these: "Is there a larger purpose for me in life?" "I'm happy most of the time, but why do I always feel that something is missing?" "Where is this feeling of emptiness and yearning coming from?" "How can I live my dreams without abandoning those I love?"

Or perhaps you're a corporate executive, a government worker, or a manager in a multinational company with a driving desire to infuse greater purpose and meaning into the workplace for your employees. You could also be a self-employed consultant, an entrepreneur, or an aspiring artist with a need to reignite your passion for your work and spirit.

Whoever you are and wherever you are in your journey to discovering greater meaning in your life and realizing your highest potential, this book was written for you. I hope you will take it along with you in your quest and use it as your personal field guide.

The Approach

I've purposely taken a no-nonsense, real-world approach to this subject because I understand that the most significant transformations we make as human beings often come from life's greatest challenges and difficulties—the grit life throws at us that becomes embedded in our soul. But just like the grain of sand that embeds itself within the oyster's shell, the grit we deal with in life can often be transformed into a beautiful pearl. This book was written to help you find that rare, one-of-a-kind pearl within you.

In this 4-week program, you will find a user-friendly format and plan of action for sharpening what I refer to as your inner guidance system. Maybe you didn't even know that you have an inner guidance system. Well, you do. And in this program you'll learn to read the various life compasses that exist within you and start putting to use a variety of practical tools and techniques for excavating and igniting the passion that will soon reveal your greater potential, talent, gifts, and higher purpose.

If you're feeling lost, this book will help you to find your way back on course, the better to see your destiny shining brightly. That's when you'll be glad to know that your True North remains a fixed point that you will come to count on for guidance in the ever-changing galaxy of your life.

Within the pages of this book, you will find a powerful course of action for navigating toward a better life. This process is outlined in 4 impactful weeks of self-discovery. *Discover True North* provides a viable toolkit that will quickly equip you to become the navigator of your own destiny.

The Power within the Collective Soul of Our Humanity

In recent years I have committed myself to developing this life-altering program, which introduces a simple, yet powerful, easy-to-understand method of personal growth and self-development within the context of what I refer to as an "emerging consciousness."

Just look around you. Men and women in every corner of the world, and the organizations they work for, are living and practicing more conscious living and doing so with greater passion and commitment to their core values. Our awareness as a human race has risen dramatically. We know now that the collective soul of our humanity can and will ultimately affect us individually somewhere down the road. And with that realization comes greater responsibility for doing the right thing because it's the right thing to do and for being the best that we can be in this lifetime.

Our quest to be all that we can be and to rise to a higher level of consciousness can be seen all around us. Collectively, companies large and small donate billions of dollars to a wide variety of humanitarian causes, both in the United States and abroad. Newman's Own, for example, donates every cent of profit from its popular food line to charity. Generous donors to a wide variety of world causes include companies like Ben & Jerry's, Amazon.com, Harpo Productions, Nissan North America, Target, Microsoft, Prudential, and others too numerous to list. In addition, ethics is being taught in top business school curricula, and environmental causes and concerns are at the head of many organizations' lists of ways to make the world a better place for tomorrow's children. One such organization is the well-known Swedish furniture company IKEA. With more than 150 stores in 29 countries, IKEA's important corporate values and philosophies are globally consistent, especially its commitment to preserving the environment through its exclusive use of building materials known to help preserve Europe's ancient forests. So what does this mean? It means that at this very moment, you and I are witnessing the most amazing transformation of higher consciousness and human development in the history of our world.

The time to bring together the best of our relationships with others and the best of our relationship with ourselves is now. I will explain this in greater detail later in the book, but for now, know that I am referring to the upgradable transformation of ourselves as human beings. All of this links us to the transformation of our work, our families, our relationships, our spirituality, and our overall humanity as we learn to better relate to and live with one another.

Purpose of This Book

My driving passion and purpose in writing this book has been to help others find more meaning, value, passion, and higher potential in both their personal and their professional lives. This passion has been cultivated over the years during my speaking tours and while conducting workshops and seminars on the power of human potential. The concept for this program was further stimulated by my work with holistic leadership behaviors and the importance of sustaining hope and morale in the workplace through intuition-based and values-led leadership.

Because of this book's down-to-earth, practical sense of personal discovery and growth, some people might call it a "how to" book. I like to think of it as also being a "what to" book: "What am I not living that wants so much to live in me?" "What should I be doing to experience the significance I long for?" "What is stopping me from pursuing my dreams and innermost desires?" "What can I do to put my talents and gifts to their best use?" This program provides specific alignment strategies for questions like these, offering you, the reader, ongoing inspiration and substance with an inside track to your own self-awareness and discovery, personal power, and enlightenment.

In this book you will be given strategies that I have field-tested time and time again in the hundreds of personal growth and human potential workshops and seminars that I've conducted worldwide for more than a decade. The result of my work is this book and the 4-week program that I call Discover True North. I am convinced that this program will ignite your passion and activate your higher potential and greater purpose.

You Are the Vessel

Although Discover True North is a dynamic and life-changing program, without the right and ready vessel, it can do nothing. I am speaking about you. You are the vessel into whom the teachings and lessons must flow so that they can be activated. As the author, I am eager to help facilitate your life-changing personal and work transformation. However, I am a great believer in intentional and accountable learning, and so the level to which you rise, the depth of meaning that you extract from the program, and the guidance that you, and you alone, choose to implement, sharpen, and apply over time are in your hands, not mine. I hold you accountable for this part of it. I am simply here to help facilitate the process with the step-by-step techniques in this book. I hope that through these engaging and motivating life tools, you will find this book to be an invaluable resource that you will draw on again and again.

I believe that you have read this far because you are serious about transforming yourself for the better, and even transforming your organization and the world around you. This is why I am inviting you to be my partner on this journey to Discover True North. We cannot and should not do this in isolation from one another. We need support and community to make this transformation long-lasting, and I will further explain how to do this later in the book.

I personally don't believe that the answers that many of us are looking for can be found either in the realm of high-tech scientific studies or through simple logic. That's why this book is different from others that you may have read. It blends the concrete, practical application of self-improvement and continuous learning with the universal laws, teachings, and traditions upon which our world was formed and continues to function. I believe it is this essential duality that sets this book and this program apart from so many others.

An Action-Driven Program

Discover True North is a program based on the concept that our soul and our inner being know, understand, and relay to us the deeper meaning and purpose of our lives. It should therefore be considered that it is our persona or personality that embodies everything that we have been born with or been given up to this point in life to enable us to reach our higher truth and purpose. How we combine the two in order to transform ourselves and move to the next level is the biggest issue and challenge that we face. This is what makes this 4-week program action-driven, rather than theory-driven. It's a program that will empower you with the necessary tools in the form of life compasses, maps, and radar for navigating your individual path, determining your talents and gifts, facing your fears, and, hence, discovering your True North.

What to Expect

My goal has been to present, in the most straightforward manner I know, four fundamental concepts for achieving life-changing results. You may want to think of each week's program as a critical building block that you can easily use at your own pace. For example, you may complete all of the exercises for Week 2 in 1 week or even less, depending on your time allowance. For other parts of the program, it may take you a month or more to fully complete all of the exercises and learning opportunities—again, this will depend on your time allowance and how you pace yourself along the way in order to make the most of each week's lessons.

In each weekly program, you will find practical methods, self-assessments, and interactive exercises to help you develop and sharpen your higher potential, along with your personal and spiritual growth quotient.

The 4 weeks of this course are divided into the following areas of self-directed study.

WEEK 1: *Do Less of What Lessens You. Do More of What Magnifies Your Soul, Your Gifts, and Your Higher Purpose*

The section for the first week focuses on the lifelong importance of strengthening your self-esteem and cultivating people and techniques that can help you to build your confidence and your authentic pride.

Healthy self-esteem is not an end goal of Discovering True North. It's an ongoing process that most of us wind up renegotiating at various stages of our lives. How we value ourselves and how we perceive our worth are two of the most powerful forces within each of us. But this power is lost if you don't tap those forces. Successfully discovering your True North hinges on breaking bad habits and no longer doing the things in life that lessen you. We've all done things that have lessened us at some point in time—maybe we've chosen the wrong friends or let someone treat us in a way that made us feel small and insignificant, or inept and unworthy.

During this week you'll discover some of the reasons that you may be lessening yourself right now and begin focusing on different ways to magnify your soul, your gifts and talents, and ultimately your higher purpose in life. If your self-esteem is in shambles, searching for your True North will prove futile. By the end of this first week, you will have tapped the power of your personal self-esteem. You will be able to identify the obstacles that threaten your confidence and combat them quickly when they arise. You will also discover helpful methods for nurturing your self-worth at home and in the workplace on a continuing basis, and you will create your own "life board of directors" in the process.

WEEK 2: *No, You Can't Be Anything You Want, but You Can Be Anything You're Capable of Becoming*

In Week 2 you'll learn how to clarify the significant differences between following one's calling and cultivating one's interests, and you'll understand why sometimes it all comes down to pacing oneself along the way. In this section of the book, you will explore techniques and real-world examples that will help you to recognize your inner voice of wisdom and courage, to take risks, and to start to really believe in who you are and what you are truly capable of becoming in this lifetime.

This is a pivotal turning point—understanding the difference between believing and wishing. You can become anything that you truly *believe* you can be, but you cannot become anything that you *wish* or *want* to be. If you grow up believing what others tell you about your place in the world, you will grow to that level and then stop growing. If you're a private pilot, but you wish that you were an astronaut instead, that won't be enough to make it a reality. However, if you grow up believing, deep inside yourself, no matter what you're told, that with the appropriate preparation and capabilities you can accomplish something greater, you will in the end become what you believe you can be. The private pilot who believes that he or she can cut the mustard in the grueling physical and mental training that's required to eventually be accepted into NASA's Astronaut Training Program has a far better shot at making that dream a reality than the private pilot who just wishes it would happen.

This week concentrates on the power of marrying your belief system with your interests, pacing yourself for success, and learning to articulate your feelings and the inner voice that tells you how to go as far as you can you can with all that you've got, and to start loving what is.

WEEK 3: *Connecting with Your Spirit without Disconnecting from Your Brain*

It is in Week 3 that you will begin to experience a more profound and personal evolution, an evolution whereby you will begin experiencing extraordinary life changes. This section places emphasis on two important criteria for living your fullest life and transforming yourself to the highest level of your potential.

One criterion is that you become a multisensory person. This is a life adjustment that you will be required to make in order to become all that you can become. In this third week of the program, you'll quickly discover that your five senses are simply not enough to get you to where you want to go, or to enable you to reach your greatest human potential and authentic power. However, when you learn to fully utilize your intuitive skills and your natural multisensory capacities, the possibilities in life and work expand.

The second criterion is that you align your inner spirit with your personality. This is often easier said than done. Remember, earlier in this preface, I related doing this to the action-driven format of this program, which is based on the concept that your inner being is wired with information that tells you more about your greater purpose in life, and that it is your personality that gives you the ability to make it all happen. Aligning the two is critical for expanding your consciousness and applying the insights you will gain to the day-to-day practices of living your life to its fullest. When these two things are out of alignment, your quest to be more cannot be fully realized.

WEEK 4: *Romancing Your Potential—Becoming an Upgradable Person*

You may frequently think of upgrading your computer system or upgrading your software program, but how often do you seriously consider upgrading yourself as a human being? Did you know, for example, that in today's global workplace, the most successful organizations have six criteria by which excellence and high performance are measured? They are doing things better, doing things faster, doing things cheaper, being more innovative, being more flexible, and—the last, but most important, criterion—hiring upgradable people! In this fourth week of the program, you'll learn what it means to romance your potential in order to upgrade your life based on the three cornerstones of higher truth and human potential: focus, service, and gratitude.

Moving into Your Equilibrium—What Life Could Be

At the conclusion of each week, I will ask you to take specific steps to clarify all that you have learned in this program. This section illustrates how to do this, using what I call the Einstein approach to calling forth your own genius. By doing this, you will learn to get around the complexities in life that hold you back and to embrace greater simplicity that will lighten your load and keep you moving forward. Moving into your equilibrium is the essence of getting it right. Everything that you will learn in this program gets simpler at the end of each week and more powerfully effective at the same time.

On a Personal Note: Feeding the Human Spirit

I have been fortunate enough to have traveled more than a million miles in my work. And from one end of the globe to the other, when speaking to audiences, whether they be in Warsaw, Poland, or in Little Rock, Arkansas, and while conducting my workshops or facilitating seminars on personal growth and improvement, I have seen and, more importantly, felt a deep-seated sense of starvation among these people. I am not referring to the kind of starvation that comes from lack of food; instead, I am referring to a different kind of world hunger—a hunger for greater soulfulness infused within people's personalities, a hunger for a more progressive and joyful path for living life and becoming an active participant and a co-creator of good in the world. This is the kind of hunger I've witnessed firsthand, a hunger that is so strong that it became the impetus for writing this book and developing this program.

It is my desire that this book will bring together your personal and professional worlds with purpose and passion. Discovering True North—a fixed point where we can become more joyful, creative, truthful, satisfied, and self-directed—will allow us to become co-creators of greater good at work, at home, and in the world—one person at a time, one day at a time, one week at a time—using this program. That's the challenge. That's the voyage. That's what I consider to be feeding the human spirit.

Acknowledgments

Before a book can become a reality, an author needs someone who believes in the idea and can envision the possibilities. In my case, that person was Nancy Hancock, executive editor at McGraw-Hill. Thank you, Nancy, for seeing this as a worthwhile project from the start and then helping shepherd my work into the world. Your insights and guidance always inspired me to do my best work. And to McGraw-Hill editor Richard Narramore, thank you for your support over the years and for introducing me to Nancy.

I'd like to give special thanks to editorial assistant Meg Leder for her attention to all the details during the editorial process. Meg, your patience and good humor helped smooth out the rough patches. I also want to thank all of the incredibly talented people at McGraw-Hill who worked on this project behind the scenes, helping to shape my manuscript into a much better book. These special people include Janice Race, senior editing supervisor. Your commitment to this book and your mindful guidance felt like a net underneath me as I leaped on to each new page. Thanks also to copy editor Alice Manning for your gifts of precious time and energy to this project, and a big thank you to Cindy LaBreacht for the composition of this book. And to my close friend and graphic specialist Elly Mixsell—a bow goes to you for generously offering your creative input and design ideas for the figures featured in this book.

Special thanks and appreciation go to my husband, David W. Thomley, for 25 years of unexpected adventure and love. Thank you for believing in me, no matter what. You are my hero, my sword, and my shield. And an immeasurable amount of my love and gratefulness goes to my daughter, Autumn Kelly Bruce. You, my daughter, are my soul print and the brightest star that shines in my True North. Thank you both for always holding me in the light of your love.

An enormous thank you goes to the thousands of people who have made up my keynote audiences around the globe, and to all of the seminar and workshop participants who believe in my programs and continue to share with me their support, their heartfelt stories, and their much-appreciated feedback. Every one of you enriches my life by allowing me to be a part of yours.

When writing a book, you rely heavily on the support and love that you get from family and friends. I am blessed with an inner circle of people who champion my work repeatedly. And although I cannot begin to thank you all individually, you know who you are, and I want you to know that it's because of you that this book got its wings.

Finally, I feel much like what Walt Whitman wrote: "As for me, I know of nothing but miracles." I thank God for my many blessings and acknowledge the Divine guidance with which I was provided to write this book.

Introduction

Right now, you are just 4 weeks away from living the life of your dreams. Just 4 weeks away from a new beginning. Just 4 weeks away from becoming the most courageous and inspired human being that you are capable of becoming.

By reading this book and subscribing to this program, you are making a conscious and deliberate commitment to focus on your personal development and to pursue your highest potential with passion. In other words, you've just made a crucial, life-altering decision. And from this point forward, every decision that you make—from accepting a promotion or relocation assignment at your job to starting a new diet, empowering yourself to leave an unhappy marriage, or nurturing your spirituality to the next level of awareness—will become a significant step toward making a greater contribution to your coworkers, your family, your friends, humanity, and, most importantly, yourself.

Are You Making the Most of Yourself?

There is a fundamental human desire to want to make a real difference in the world. There is also a basic human need for significance and meaningful purpose. We are reminded, in the words of Ralph Waldo Emerson, to "Make the most of yourself . . . for that is all there is of you." How are you making the most of yourself? This is a question that I pose to audiences at the end of one of my keynote speeches. When I ask this question to audiences as large as 1000 or more people, the silence is deafening.

Afterwards, I am frequently approached by people from those audiences who want to know, "How can I make the most of myself?" This is the one question that I am asked more than any other.

If you too are asking this question, I am betting that there are two things going on in your life right now. First, you are seeking greater meaning in what your life is about and where you are headed or what you are destined to do in this lifetime. You may be unhappy or disillusioned with your current circumstances, at home, at work, or both, and have a strong desire to find a more gratifying and fulfilling path—a need to get into alignment with your True North. Second, you feel your inner self, your soul, the essence of who you are deep down, calling out to you—yearning for something greater and more meaningful that up to this point you have felt unable to provide. If this is the case, I'm suggesting that you give yourself the time you need to nurture yourself, first and foremost.

Before going any further, let me add something right here. It is not selfish to focus on yourself first, before others, when you are embracing this kind of self-development program. I'm not suggesting that you abandon your loved ones or ignore your family and friends' needs. What I'm saying is that when you focus on your ultimate vision and life goal, or, as Emerson says, on "making the most of yourself," you are demonstrating that you are honoring something greater than yourself, and when you do this, I guarantee that in the long run you will have much more, and will be far better equipped, to give back to the people in your life who need you most.

Necessary as the Oxygen You Breathe

Making the most of yourself requires that ongoing self-development and self-nurturing be as necessary to you as the oxygen you breathe. An everyday analogy for this comes from all the air travel required in my work. No matter how many hundreds of thousands of miles I have flown in my lifetime, the flight crew never ceases to underscore the importance of placing the oxygen mask on myself first should there be a drop in cabin pressure, before assisting anyone else. The point is that you are no good to anyone else if you are incapacitated, tired, worn out, or depleted of spiritual fulfillment and purposefulness, whether the problem be lack of oxygen or failure to fulfill a higher purpose and create meaning in your life. So if you truly intend to make the most of yourself, then give something back to yourself —starting with this program—and see what happens.

Be the Primary Navigator in Your Life

In order for you to gain the most from this book, it is imperative that you agree to take charge and become the primary navigator in your life. That means that you chart the course. You take the wheel and steer. Therefore, I am asking that you begin by agreeing to the following three life-changing commitments that will serve to place you on the right course—a course that gets results—and put you in the right mindset for getting the most out of this program:

1. *Make your personal growth and self-development a top priority.* This means that you must stop worrying about what others think about you or your personal quest to discover your True North. It means that you must stop living your life for other people. Translation: Stop seeking the approval of others before pursuing your passion and your dreams and putting your higher gifts and talents to use (your greater purpose for being here). Be prepared. When you start practicing the principles in this program, others whom you know may cast their votes against you. Surprised? Don't be. It's not unusual for so-called friends to be the first to rise and tell you what you cannot achieve and whom you cannot become. After all, if you succeed, you will be exceeding the expectations they always had for you. How to deflect your fears and self-doubt in moments of weakness is part of what you'll be learning.

2. *Use your intellect and your faith in tandem.* Trust your intelligence and your innate ability to reason and let that reinforce the wisdom that you already have inside you, along with the capability to adjust and set new priorities and goals in your life. Next, focus on maintaining your faith or rediscovering the faith that you have lost. Trust that your faith and your belief in something greater than what you're capable of contemplating will guide you through life's uncharted and turbulent waters when you need it most. To succeed in this program, it is important that you retain your faith in both yourself and a greater power, and that no matter what difficulties this world may impose, as you awaken to your greater potential and discover your True North, the great mystery of your life will unfold perfectly in alignment with the universal laws of greater truth and understanding. When we embrace both intellect and faith, we experience the power of human flexibility—the flexibility for handling whatever might come our way. In his book *Living on Purpose,* Dan Millman says that by "living on purpose and acting on principle we become like bamboo—strong yet supple—yielding to the forces we encounter, then snapping back on track." This is a powerful metaphor from which we can all learn and profit.

3. *Focus on the present and start living forward.* I'm not saying that you should ignore the past. Examining and talking about our life experiences, good and bad, can be greatly revealing and therapeutic. What I mean here is, don't allow yourself to get permanently stuck in some of the key developmental moments of your life. This happens when we spend an unbalanced amount of time

looking back, dwelling on what was and what cannot be changed, what could have been or should have happened, or poring over our childhoods again and again, digging up the past and all the feelings that go with it.

What I'm suggesting here is that you start applying two very important universal principles. First, focus on the present and be fully aware of every moment that is happening to you here and now. And second, develop a vision of the future and the possibilities of your life by getting off the road from the past. When you do this, you will add a whole new dimension to the process of developing your greater potential and the talents and gifts you were born to use. Think about it. These are the basic principles of staying focused and living forward that have been practiced in cultures all over the world for thousands of years. The Greeks considered those who followed their dreams and visions the most courageous of all human beings. The ancient Egyptians worshipped the phoenix, the mythical bird that rose, reborn, from its own ashes. For centuries, Native Americans have pursued change and transformation through vision quest rituals and intense isolation, and many Eastern religions use the practices of meditation and forward thinking to this same end.

When we live forward with vision for a better tomorrow, we equip ourselves with the natural power to fully appreciate our future endeavors and accomplishments. We start to dwell in the possibilities that can transform us.

Purposeful Ways to Use This Book

I have spent a great deal of time deciding on the best way to make the format of these pages and the learning within them purposeful. Because I have more than 15 years of training and program design experience, I have formatted the lessons in this book for different adult learning styles, all of which provide easy access for the transfer and application of this navigational system to your life.

Acknowledging Your Higher Purpose Statement

Each chapter of this book begins with an interactive higher purpose statement. I will provide you with a statement and give you specific instructions for responding to it. Each statement has a powerful connection to a bigger picture, a larger vision, and the start of a new life strategy. Your ongoing interactive involvement will bring the bigger picture closer to reality and make it more adaptable to your specific and life-changing needs as you move through the program.

Throughout this book, I will include relevant real-world stories that help to underscore particular learning points, sidebars for fast information, and inspirational quotes that enhance each section's theme. Also, you will find in each chapter a myriad of tools, tips, resources, models, checklists, and self-assessments, plus a step-by-step program for finding your inner guidance system in order to build self-esteem and live more authentically through self-empowerment and inner growth.

Moving into Your Equilibrium

Maintaining your equilibrium while going through this program is key. I'll discuss this more later in the book, but for now, know that keeping your balance as you take in this information will help you to retain the information and learn faster. At the end of each week I will ask you to repeat four important steps that will move you into your equilibrium for higher learning.

STEP 1: *Stop and Breathe*

This is the easiest of the four steps. All it requires of you is that you take a few moments to stop whatever you are doing, take a few deep breaths, and slowly release them. That's it. Just stop and breathe. Clear your mind and reflect on what it is you have just learned. At this stage, don't worry about how you will apply what you've learned; that will come later. For now, just take a few minutes to concentrate solely on the lessons you have gleaned from this section of the program. Concentrate on how those lessons apply to you, how they might enhance and enlighten your life, and how they might give you more confidence or greater feelings of inspiration. Then take a moment to simply appreciate that you have gained a new perspective, perhaps even a higher perspective, on something that is important to your passion and your higher potential. This first step is one of reflection and inner peace, letting go and focusing on what matters most at that moment.

STEP 2: *Be Conscious and Think*

Earlier in the book, I spoke of an emerging consciousness. Here's one example: Spiritual living used to be the focus and passion of just a handful of people, but with today's emerging consciousness, it is now the interest of many. What was once considered a personal quest is now integrated into people's work, graduate business courses, and personal relationships at every level. That's the potency of consciousness. The difficulty often lies in how vigilant we are when it comes to listening to that consciousness.

For example, the collective viewpoint about our personal safety in the world that we once adopted has been radically affected by global terrorism. Shortly after the attacks on the World Trade Center and the Pentagon took place, people's focus on their safety and the safety of others was sharp. However, less than a year after the attacks took place, and even though warnings of the inevitability of future attacks remained high, it was evident that people were far less conscious of the possibility of harm. People were much more relaxed about the issues of terror and somewhat disconnected from their own unconscious awareness of what could happen. One woman in Austin, Texas, told me after a workshop that New York and Washington, D.C., were not part of her world, so why should she worry. I don't think this woman is an isolated case. The higher level of consciousness that existed closer to September 11 has waned considerably.

To this day, when I board an aircraft, no matter where I am, I am fully aware of what is going on around me. What concerns me deeply is that some of the people on the airplane may not be fully attentive to their safety, and their behaviors often show it. I often say to myself, "Who's thinking here?" "Who's aware?"

As you work through this program, it is essential that you continue to hone your consciousness about living life in general and that you keep your awareness level high and activated. I'm not just talking about airport safety or the threat of terrorism. I'm referring to taking part in conscious day-to-day living—self-awareness and the awareness of all that goes on around you, from the sun outside your office window to the smell of coffee in the morning. Open your eyes. Pay attention. And think. In the words of Maya Angelou, "It's time for thinking people to start thinking." Angelou also says, "Now that we know better, we must do better." I can't think of a better directive when it comes to living your life in a way that makes the best use of your personal empowerment and accountability.

STEP 3: *Choose and Commit*

As much as this is a book about personal transformation, it is also a book about making life choices and committing to something in this world that is larger than the obvious day-to-day realities and life routines.

If you don't take charge of your life, someone else will. Therefore, this program requires that you be an active participant—someone who takes charge of living her or his life to the fullest, isn't afraid to make choices and then act on those choices. Our faith in something larger than ourselves gives us the power to create a larger vision and purpose for our lives. It also reminds us that every decision we make leads us to a newer and stronger inner wisdom. Here is how.

You and I are not going to make infallible life choices; everything will not work out every time we make a decision. Our lives are about learning and self-discovery. And besides, how bad are wrong decisions? So what if you make a wrong choice? The world will not collapse as a result. Looking back, we've all made choices that have caused us heartache or setbacks, but the chances are good that we learned something invaluable from those experiences. The point is that taking the easier path, the path of least resistance, may not be the better choice after all.

I'm here to tell you that it's time to look at all your life choices from a higher perspective. I like to call this "helicopter thinking." The choices we make—good or not—just lead us down one path or another. But regardless of the road you take, every road leads to a new lesson, and every lesson leads to a new inner strength and inner wisdom. So whatever choice you make at the moment is the perfect choice for you at that very moment in time. And life is made up of moments in time. The key is to act on your deepest truth as each moment presents itself. The flip side is that it's perfectly all right to change your mind!

STEP 4: *Act and Then Move toward Something*

This is probably the most critical of the four steps that I am requesting you to take at the end of each week's lessons. The fact is, if you are waiting for permission to act on your desires, if you are holding back until things get easier or until you feel more motivated and less fearful, or if you're simply waiting for hell to freeze over, stop right here and go no further. I'm here to tell you that the "perfect moment" will never come and that the action of taking no action is likely to become your passion's undoing.

The Two Constants in Life

The reality of self-help is that there are actually only two things you *have* to do in this life. First, you will someday *have* to leave this life, this body you inhabit, and this world we live in. And second, you and you alone are the only one who *has* to live your life until you are gone. That's it. The rest we somehow create along the way. How you choose to create your life, develop your career, cherish your relationships, find new courage, build your self-esteem, eliminate the fear of what others may think, and be accountable for everything that you have become up to this point is the transformation upon which you are about to embark.

It is my hope that you will find this book to be a valuable hands-on guide for unleashing your deepest passion and then claiming the life you were born to live by doing something with it, starting today.

WEEK
1

Do Less of What Lessens You.
Do More of What Magnifies
Your Soul, Your Gifts, and
Your Higher Purpose

1

If You're Going to Compromise, Compromise Up!

Higher Purpose Statement

Never function below the level of your potential or settle for less when you deserve more. When you do, you compromise your chances of reaching your True North. Don't hide from the risks of growing yourself. When you do, you compromise your greater purpose in life. Never make failure a reason to compromise your resolve and commitment to what you believe in and stand for. Never compromise the opportunities that life gives you to enrich yourself at higher levels. Each time you do this, you give away a piece of your soul and chip away at your identity. From this moment forward, make an agreement with yourself that whenever you find you are in a position that calls for compromise, you will compromise up. Your authentic self rests on what you stand for and on being true to yourself. Expect more, not less. When you compromise up, you raise the bar on life, and that's a good thing.

Discovering Your True North Requires Compromising Up

When buffalo roamed North America, it was the light of Polaris—the North Star—that guided the nomadic Plains Indian tribes. Through the centuries, explorers and mariners have depended on the never-altering North Star as a fixed point in the night sky when no other landmarks or navigational instruments were available. While all the other stars in the sky continue to move from east to west, Polaris does not move, but remains a steady nighttime compass of guidance, light, and dependability.

I believe that we all have within us our own Polaris, or True North, a fixed inner compass that we can look to for safe and reliable guidance when we feel we have lost our way. This book was written to help you discover your own True North—that navigational star that shines within you. However, as you journey toward your inner compass, you will be faced with a multitude of life choices along the way—choices that will either draw you nearer to finding your True North or pull you further away from this amazing inner light.

When you acknowledge and honor your True North, you are saying that you believe that within you lie the answers that will give you greater happiness and higher potential, ignite your passions, and allow you to live your dreams—in short, the answers to living the life you were born to live, a life in which you compromise up and stop selling yourself short.

I believe that the relationship between our Northern Hemisphere and the North Star is very similar to the relationship between you and your True North, or your higher purpose—the reason you are here to begin with.

There may be times when you feel utterly alone—lost and even without hope. But when you discover your True North, as you are about to do in this book, you will soon locate and then unleash a powerful life tool to call upon when you need it most—a dependable and accurate compass that you can count on to always bring you back to that fixed point of who you really are: your authentic self, among the ever-evolving constellations of your life. If you are to discover your True North, you must compromise up and willingly accept into your life the best that life has to offer.

If You Want to Compromise Up, You've Got to Raise Your Standards

When I talk about compromising up, please don't misunderstand my intentions. I'm not referring to material gain or to feeding an insatiable hunger for acquiring more things—another car, a faster boat, a bigger diamond ring, a larger house in a more exclusive neighborhood. If you have all these things and you are living a happy and fulfilling life, then you are blessed beyond measure. But so often, when people crave more and more things in their lives, it stems from a kind of spiritual deprivation and diminished sense of self-worth. In my workshops, we discuss why some people have a need to be defined by their material possessions, rather than being defined by who they are and what they stand for.

One more thing: Let me be perfectly clear about the important message in this chapter. When I talk about compromising up, I'm not saying that you should act like a diva, be insensitive to others' needs, behave rudely, or expect to get your own way in all situations. I'm simply saying that you should *raise your standards* to a higher level so that you can create the healthiest emotional and physical environment in which you can thrive, be your best self, and live your best life. In my seminars, I call these Platinum Standards for Abundant Living. I will explain this in greater depth later in this chapter.

First, let's look at how we do or don't help to create an environment in which we can thrive. I believe this is more an issue of self-esteem than it is an issue of compromise, and I will discuss this further in Chapter 3. But for now, you need to know that standing up for yourself and wanting better—not settling for less, but expecting the magnificent rather than the mediocre, the great rather than the good—is not selfish by any means. Rather, expecting the best for yourself is an extension of your self-worth and the level of esteem in which you hold yourself. It also is a reflection of the standards by which you live your life and the things in life that you feel you are worthy of receiving.

Accepting Less for Ourselves, Expecting More for Others

So why do we regularly accept less for ourselves, but expect, and even encourage, more for others? Maybe it's because we are taught so often to accept less, or to put the needs of others ahead of our own. In my workshops on building self-esteem, the words I hear over and over again are things like "I don't like to make a scene," "I'd prefer not to rock the boat," "I never send food back that I've ordered in a restaurant, no matter how badly it's cooked," "I didn't leave the relationship because I believed I wouldn't find someone better," "I stayed in a job I hated because I didn't have enough faith in myself to try out my God-given talents in a job I really wanted," or "I wish I could feel more confident standing up for myself, but I don't." I could give you hundreds of examples.

Compromising up, treating yourself with greater respect, and living by higher standards shows the world that you respect yourself and that you deserve more, not less, in your life. It also speaks to the value that you place on your time and energy.

Are Your Time and Energy Being Soaked Up by Life's Mediocre?

Two of the most valuable resources we possess as human beings are our time and our energy. How you honor these two precious resources is a direct reflection on the kind of people and circumstances that you allow into your life, or the choices you make.

When you compromise down or settle for less, I guarantee that you will get just that and no more. But when you make an honest attempt to get what you truly deserve by compromising up, you gain the respect and admiration of others, and you attract the best that life can offer because you think enough of yourself not to just accept the mediocre that life dishes out.

Are You Distancing Yourself from True North?

How often do you compromise your standards by settling for less in life? Do you allow certain people to treat you poorly or with disrespect? Have you ever settled for lower quality in an item that you purchased because you didn't want to complain? Have you accepted something that fell short of what you asked for and not attempted to correct the situation? Whenever we allow ourselves to be treated this way and accept what is instead of what could be, we are making choices that further distance us from our True North and the life we deserve—a life of self-respect and honor.

When We Fail to Compromise Up

Here are three real-world examples taken from different workshops I've led (names have been changed) showing what can happen and how our lives take shape, moving us further from True North, when we fail to compromise up:

> ➤ Josh purchased a digital video camera at a reputable and well-known electronics store. Just 2 days after he bought the camera, one of the programming functions stopped working reliably. Josh convinced himself that the retailer would have frowned on a return or refund, since this had been the last camera in stock, so he talked himself into accepting the lower-quality item for which he had paid full price. He told himself that he'd just make do and take his chances with the programming function, or use his friend's digital video camera when there was something important that he wanted to record. Clearly Josh lacked the nerve to approach the retailer from which he had purchased the faulty equipment and ask for what he rightly deserved—a new camera or a refund. Instead, Josh settled for less, and that's exactly what he got.

> ➤ Laura and her husband, Jeff, had been hearing about a great new seafood restaurant in the city. There was lots of buzz about the restaurant's chef and his special lobster creations. So they decided to give it a try on their tenth

wedding anniversary. For dinner, Laura ordered the house specialty, a lobster and pasta dish, and was disappointed. The lobster was barely warm, and the pasta was overcooked. Also, Laura had specified that she didn't want garlic in her dish, and there was lots of garlic. On top of all this, the à la carte dish cost $45. When Laura's husband sensed that she was dissatisfied, he offered to ask their server to correct the problem, but Laura objected. She tried to convince her husband that the problem was no big deal and that she could live with the cold, limp, garlicky seafood dinner. Obviously, Laura felt intimidated by the restaurant's tony surroundings and formal-looking waitstaff. She was sure that their waiter would be angry at her disapproval of the meal—after all, no one else seemed to be complaining. Laura settled for less, and that's exactly what she got.

➤ Meg's mother fell seriously ill and was hospitalized. Although the hospital had received a high ranking for medical treatment, consistent patient care was another story. Meg felt that the hospital staff seemed cold and insensitive. The duty nurse assigned to her mother's floor was a man who was easily irritated by the smallest request, and the hospital admitting office was rude and short with Meg when she admitted her mother, even though it was clear that Meg was distracted and concerned about her mother's condition. When the night shift started and the same ill-tempered nurse snapped at Meg's mother for requesting an additional blanket for her bed, Meg stood by in disbelief as her mother, looking hurt and angry, recoiled with tears in her eyes. But Meg said nothing. She later consoled her mother for what had happened, but she never addressed the issue with the nurse himself or his supervisor.

Meg's own insecurity about speaking up on behalf of her mother made her feel that if she said something about her mother's poor treatment, the entire nursing staff would be angry with her, and then what? She'd have to face these people every day, and that would be too uncomfortable to bear. Meg settled for less when it came to her mother's hospital care, and that's what her mother received.

The Power of Choice Drastically Changes the Path You Travel toward True North

What is it that Josh, Laura, and Meg all have in common? For starters, each one is allowing life's mediocre treatment of them to soak up their two greatest resources:

time and energy. All of them need to raise their standards and stop accepting the best of the worst life has to offer. Josh, Laura, and Meg need to face this life-altering choice if they are to travel a path to True North. The choice is clear: *abundance* over *self-deprivation*.

NAVIGATION TOOL: *Choosing Abundance over Self-Deprivation*

Josh could have easily taken the digital video camera back to the retail store. It was known for high-quality customer service, and it would gladly have replaced the camera with something commensurate or given him a full refund. Had he done this, how different would his life be? More than likely, Josh would have felt proud of himself for having spoken up and ultimately getting what he rightfully deserved—a product that was not defective. He wouldn't have to further inconvenience himself by borrowing a friend's camera for the "important" videos he wanted to shoot, soaking up more time and energy along the way. By choosing abundance over self-deprivation, Josh would change his life significantly. He would be compromising up, living the life he deserved, and feeling better about himself as a man.

And what about Laura? You can bet this wasn't the first substandard meal she had eaten and paid for in a restaurant. Even though she was fully entitled to have a lovely meal with her husband on their tenth anniversary, Laura didn't think enough of herself to allow that to happen.

How different would Laura's life be if she had just spoken up for herself? For starters, she would almost immediately have been treated with greater respect. Laura never gave her server the benefit of the doubt by allowing him to correct the problem for her, thereby giving him the opportunity to please his customer and feel good about himself. Instead, Laura took that decision away from the server and *chose* to play the victim role, as her family has witnessed time and again.

If Laura would only learn to stand up for herself, she would be setting a much better example for her children, and she would be treated with greater respect and dignity by others. Compromising up and choosing abundance over self-deprivation would greatly improve the quality of Laura's life.

And what about Meg? By not speaking up to the rude and insensitive nurse the first time around, Meg actually contributed to her mother's mistreatment. By not asking the nurse to step outside to discuss her concerns, but instead making the decision to let it go, Meg gave the nurse permission to continue with the poor and disrespectful treatment of her mother. We teach people how to treat us, and that's exactly what Meg was unintentionally doing in this case and in many situations before this one.

How might Meg's life take a different turn if she would just be honest with others and stand up for herself and her family? For starters, in this situation, her mother would have received higher-quality patient care right from her hospital admittance. Meg would have been setting the tone for what is and is not acceptable treatment of her family.

By speaking up for her mother's rights, Meg would have gained credibility among the hospital staff as a concerned and observant daughter, increasing the probability that action would have been taken to correct the problems early on. Meg also would have been sending a strong message to the hospital staff that said, "I'm paying attention to what's going on here, and I will continue to monitor the quality of my mother's care, because I expect more." If Meg starts compromising up, she will drastically alter her path toward True North and enrich her family's life with greater abundance.

In all three of these cases, Josh, Laura, and Meg made life choices for their individual situations. Each of them chose self-deprivation over abundance. And when we choose self-deprivation over abundance, we choose to alter our life's course, moving us further away from, not closer to, our True North.

We Are Where We Are Because of the Choices We Make

Whenever you allow fear, intimidation, lack of control, and low self-worth to be a part of the choices you make in life, you are automatically choosing a life of self-deprivation. You've *chosen* to compromise down.

Know this: Living a life of self-deprivation in no way makes you a more generous person, as some might have you believe. In fact, it works just the opposite. Being a martyr or a victim is not giving and thoughtful behavior by any stretch of the imagination. The more you deprive yourself of a life of emotional and physical well-being, the more selfish and self-absorbed you become.

But when you speak up for yourself, demonstrate your confidence, ask for what you deserve, act with conviction, expect more rather than less, and take a stand for something, you will automatically be choosing a life of greater abundance. You will be compromising up and moving on a path that gravitates closer to your internal True North.

Are You Moving Closer to or Further Away from Your True North?

LIFE COMPASS: *Self-Assessment*

Complete the following exercise by ranking your behavioral tendencies with a checkmark on a scale from *never* to *almost always*. The closer you are to checking *never* in your responses, the closer you are to finding True North. The closer your checkmark is to *almost always*, the further you are from reaching True North. At a glance, the scale provides a quick self-assessment for determining the frequency and type of the life choices you are currently making.

NEVER	SOME-TIMES	ALMOST ALWAYS	
———	———	———	I often compromise my standards when I am in a situation that makes me feel uncomfortable.
———	———	———	I allow certain people to treat me poorly and with disrespect.
———	———	———	I settle for lower quality in items that I purchase because I feel uncomfortable complaining.
———	———	———	I rarely stand up for myself if someone puts me down or tries to take advantage of me.
———	———	———	I think I'll speak up to voice my opinion when necessary, but then I never do.
———	———	———	I feel that some of my choices stem from fear and intimidation, rather than from self-confidence.
———	———	———	I give away my power to others.
———	———	———	I feel deprived of self-respect.
———	———	———	I feel a lack of abundance in my life.
———	———	———	I rarely take time to honor myself and my life standards.
———	———	———	I sometimes feel that I'm not living my most authentic life.
———	———	———	I make choices that deprive me of living my best life.
———	———	———	I gravitate toward the mediocre but crave better.

Explanation: If you place a checkmark under *sometimes* or *almost always*, that area should be considered an area for self-improvement and ongoing development. For personal growth and development, complete the following exercises. Then reassess yourself in 3 weeks, using this diagnostic. Note the areas that you have worked to improve and continue the process until you check *never* for all the statements.

Declare What You Stand For

Soon I am going to have you develop your own list of Platinum Standards for Abundant Living. But first, I want you to create a Life Mission Statement and let it become your personal mantra and your declaration of who you are and what you stand for. There's an old saying that goes, "Stand for something, or fall for anything." If you don't declare what it is that you stand for in life, then who will?

Organizations spend bundles of money on management consultants to help them create corporate mission statements—some of which are empty phrases that few people can remember or recite when asked. And yet, the people in the organization—who are its soul and its greatest capital asset—rarely take time to declare their own Life Mission Statement. Is it any wonder that organizations all over the world lack soulfulness because they are out of alignment with the needs and desires of the people who keep them in business, or that employee morale is at an all-time low? None of us can perform at our highest potential if we are expected to behave in ways that are inconsistent with how we really see ourselves. (See more on this in Chapter 5.)

To help you get started, here is an example of one person's Life Mission Statement shared at one of my seminars.

> My mission is to live my best life according to my highest values and standards. I strive daily to live a life of greater purpose, while developing my highest potential and God-given gifts. I make my emotional, physical, and spiritual well-being my top priority so that I may serve others and give of myself more generously. I compromise up when faced with life choices, big and small. I ask for what I deserve. I take a stand, and I expect more because I know that is what I deserve. I choose to live an abundant, happy, and authentic life and to pass this philosophy on to my children.

Now it is your turn. Complete the following exercise. Write your own Life Mission Statement. By doing this, you will be creating a valuable life compass that you will use again and again when navigating toward True North. Make it reflect what you stand for and what you believe in. After you have written your statement, test its authenticity. Ask yourself, "Is this really who I am? Do I behave in alignment with this statement, or do I act in contradiction of it? Is this what I believe? Is this what

I stand for?" These questions and your answers provide the criteria necessary for knowing that you have created an honest and authentic Life Mission Statement.

When you have completed this exercise, you will have laid the foundation from which you will make a variety of life choices, big and small, calibrating your life compass along the way as you move toward your higher, more authentic self.

LIFE COMPASS: *My Personal Mission Statement*

_____

_____

_____

_____

_____

Creating Platinum Standards for Abundant Living

When you establish and live by your highest standards, you honor your True North—the essence of who you are and what you are all about.

There are no right or wrong ways of setting higher life standards. They are yours and yours alone. Make a list that reflects the best of you. To help you get started, I've provided a few examples from some of my seminar participants in the past. Maybe some of their higher standards will help jog your own thinking.

> ➤ I place great value on my time and my energy.

> ➤ I define myself by who I am, not by what I have.

> ➤ I don't allow self-defeating behaviors to chip away at my self-esteem.

> ➤ I am not afraid to speak up or to stand up for myself when it's called for.

> ➤ I compromise up whenever possible.

> ➤ I make choices, big and small, that are in alignment with my Platinum Standards.

➤ I believe that my talents are a gift that I am responsible for using to my fullest ability.

➤ I choose abundant living over self-deprivation.

➤ I give my respect to others and expect the same in return.

➤ I trust that my True North will provide me with the reliable guidance I am seeking, and so I continue to move toward it and the essence of who I am.

LIFE COMPASS: *Create Your Own List of Platinum Standards*

Review the list of Platinum Standards I've provided for you. Which of these standards might you consider incorporating into your own life? Now list your own Platinum Standards here. Share your ideas with others who are participating in the program. Ask for input from others, then watch your life's standards rise up.

➤ _____

➤ _____

➤ _____

➤ _____

➤ _____

➤ _____

➤ _____

➤ _____

After you've created your list, go back and, for each standard you have selected, respond to the following question: How do I prove it?

By answering this question for each and every Platinum Standard you have listed, you will be holding yourself accountable for taking action and living the standards in your daily life. This is important, because without action, standards are meaningless.

Watch how your Platinum Standards can quickly become a reliable barometer for many of life's choices.

For example, the people you allow into your life should always inspire your best work and give you every opportunity to honor your higher purpose, encouraging you closer to your True North. If you begin to question whether the people around you support your desire to live your best life, refer back to your Platinum Standards. Are these people and their behaviors and intentions in alignment with your higher standards and principles for living a more abundant life? For more on how to determine this, see Chapter 2.

Referring to your Platinum Standards works for smaller life choices, too. Let's say you're about to choose a movie to go see. Is the message that movie sends going to fuel your intellect or your emotional well-being? Nurture your nature. Be sensitive to both the positive and the detrimental effects you might experience from a wide variety of media that you let into your life—from movies, books, and music to television programs, magazines you subscribe to, and even the Internet. When you've set Platinum Standards for yourself, you start paying closer attention to all the things you allow to enter your mind and leave impressions there. You can quickly filter some of these choices, and determine what serves you best, by asking yourself these four questions before making a final decision about something:

1. Will the choice I am making honor my higher purpose and move me closer to True North?

2. Is this choice in alignment with my Platinum Standards, allowing me to live a more abundant and fulfilling life?

3. Does the choice I am making honor my two most precious resources—my time and my energy?

4. Am I choosing to accept into my life the best of the best, rather than the best of the worst?

I suspect that your gut reaction will help you answer these questions immediately, and if the answer to each one isn't a resounding *yes!* then you may need to further examine your motivation for making the choices you are making and to question why you continue to allow the mediocre, rather than the magnificent, to creep into your life. Shifting our paradigms on how we make choices takes time. So be patient. Don't beat yourself up for needing more time to adjust to this new way of thinking and to living by new and higher life standards.

Shifting Paradigms to Living a More Abundant Life

When you choose to live a life of abundance and bounty, you are choosing to live a life of greater love, generosity, public spirit, service, forgiveness, benevolence, and unselfishness. Getting to this point seldom requires anything less than making significant paradigm shifts in your thinking processes.

You will be honoring your Platinum Standards for Abundant Living when you compromise up and model the higher standards you have adopted by living and demonstrating them in your actions on a daily basis.

Getting started, however, will take some work and some shifting of old patterns of behavior that you've been holding on to all these years—patterns that may be holding you back from reaching Polaris.

To help you shift your paradigm of behavior from self-deprivation to abundant living, I've designed an Abundant Living Model that simplifies the overall concept and illustrates the process (see Figure 1-1).

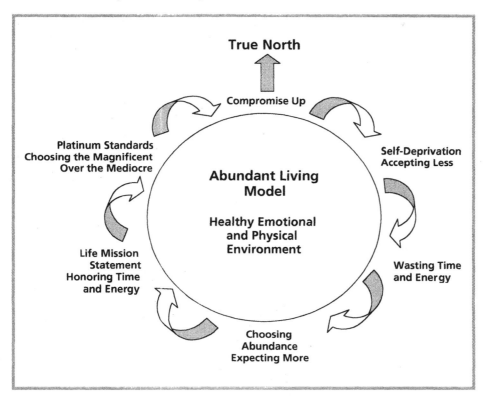

Figure 1-1. Shifting Our Paradigms from Self-Deprivation to Abundant Living

As you prepare to move on to the next chapter, I have some questions for you. Do you believe that you have the courage and convictions necessary to live a life of abundance rather than self-deprivation? Are you ready to start compromising up by inviting more into your life and by co-creating, with something far greater than yourself, an environment that is rich in both emotional and physical well-being? Will you stop settling for less, when you know you deserve better? If you've answered yes to all three questions, you are ready to move on to the lessons in the next chapter.

Sure there will be moments when you are tempted to go back to your old habits and accept less than what you deserve. When that happens, just stop right there. Don't be hard on yourself. Take the time to praise yourself for how far you have come and to acknowledge the times when you have compromised up, fully appreciating that if you did it once, you can do it again.

Just know that as you continue to practice making choices that honor your highest standards, there is a greater force than you at work—a higher power that compels you to move forward toward the essence of who you are and what you stand for: your True North.

2

Cultivate People Who Feed Your Soul —Create a Life Board of Directors

Higher Purpose Statement

Reevaluate the company that you keep. Avoid people who lead lives of hopelessness and quiet desperation. Actively seek out and gravitate toward like-minded people and people who are greater and more successful than yourself. Be true to the wisdom of your highest inner counsel—your most trustworthy built-in guide and navigator.

Here's a promise: If you subscribe to and practice this higher purpose statement, you will be putting into place a powerful self-honoring strategy that can transform your life and your ability to travel a higher path of meaning and purpose. It's time for you to take back your power and gain the level of confidence necessary to make your greatest contribution to the world.

Shrinking for the Sake of Others

How often do you become small or less significant for the sake of others? Once a day? Twice a day? Every week? Every month? There is nothing powerful or enlightening about shrinking your desires, your passions, and your vision so that others around you can feel less insecure about themselves. Nevertheless, this is a common trap of human behavior. Avoiding this trap is one of the greatest lessons of discovering True North.

If you've been apologizing for your dreams, it's time for you to stop and come to grips with the reality that, yes, there are people you know, people you love, and people you call friends who don't feel good about themselves and are not at the same level of personal growth and awareness that you are at right now. Having said that, you may have to accept the idea that your quest for a higher purpose in life may very well bring out the worst in some people, even people who genuinely care about you.

Who Do You Think You Are?

We all have been in situations where we *felt* a question and a sense of doubt hanging in the air around us. You may have felt it even when the other person didn't actually come out and say the words: "Who do you think you are?"

This is what I call the *destructive self-doubt question*. It is the question that stops all of us dead in our tracks, fills our minds with doubt, and makes us second-guess what we know in our hearts. Why? Because when someone poses that question to us, or even thinks it about us, it strikes at the very core of our own insecurities and inhibitions. It's so potent that you actually feel the distinct and definite attitude that it radiates the moment someone implies that you're incapable of doing what you say you're going to do.

There's another uncomfortable feeling that you may get when you're around certain people. It happens especially when something really great occurs in your life—for example, you get a big promotion or you buy a new house—and it contains an even stronger message: "How dare you exceed my expectations of who I think you should be and what I think you are capable of accomplishing." It doesn't matter whether people are merely thinking these things or saying them out loud. The point is, they are sending out an energy that is deliberately trying to bring you down to their level. What are you doing to stop it?

You can try to push these attitudes and thoughts out of your mind when they happen, you can deny that they're happening until the cows come home, and you can even talk yourself into blaming yourself for doing or saying something that brings out the jealous side of people. But the reality remains: Many of the people with whom you have surrounded yourself during your life may have a very difficult time accepting the fact that you are, indeed, exceeding their expectations. And it doesn't matter whether you think these people should or shouldn't feel threatened. One woman said to me in a workshop, "But she's my best friend. I would do anything for her. There's no reason for Louise to feel threatened by anything that I accomplish." My immediate thought was: "Yes, your best friend could feel threatened and probably does."

Never Diminish Your Light for the Sake of Someone Else's Low Self-Esteem

Marianne Williamson puts it best when she says, "It is our light, not our darkness that frightens people." I like what Williamson is saying because it underscores the critical importance of recognizing that when you diminish your light of higher potential and greatness for the purpose of placating someone else, you are actually lessening yourself.

Sometimes our greatest fear is not that we will prove to be inadequate or inferior, but that we will actually become more powerful, more intelligent, more perceptive, and more brilliant than we can now imagine. And if that happens, what next? How will your life change? How will all this affect the personal and professional relationships in your life? What will people think of you? Will people say, "Who do you think you are?" And will you care?

NAVIGATION TOOL: *Stop! Take Time to Identify Patterns of Your Behavior That May Be Lessening You*

Stop here. Get some paper and start writing now. Recall a time in your life when you dimmed your light for the sake of someone else's low self-esteem. What triggered the situation that made you respond by lessening yourself to appease others? How did it make you feel about yourself? How did it make you feel about the people involved? Do you see a pattern of consistent behavior in which some of the company you keep may be trying to hold you back or bring you down? Now contemplate and respond to the questions I mentioned earlier:

How will your life change if you become more powerful, more intelligent, more perceptive, and more brilliant than ever? And if that happens, what next? How will your life change?

How will all this affect the personal and professional relationships in your life?

What will people think of you? Will people say, "Who do you think you are?" And will you care?

Your responses to these questions will make up one of the most critical of the navigational compasses within your inner guidance system. This compass will help guide you back to your True North whenever you find yourself in a similar situation.

Resisting the Judgment of Others

Once you've committed to making the most of yourself and creating a larger vision and purpose for your life, something phenomenal begins to emerge from within you. All of a sudden you realize that your dreams, your vision, and your life can now be defined in your own terms and no one else's, and that from this point forward you have to resist abiding by the judgments of others.

> "Our worst fear is not that we are inadequate, our deepest fear is that we are powerful beyond measure."
> —NELSON MANDELA

There is absolutely no way that you will ever be able to satisfy the critics and naysayers that life brings to your door. Throughout your lifetime, there will always be those who try to bring you down and lessen you. It then becomes your choice whether or not to engage them. I suggest that you pass and do less of what lessens you and more of what magnifies your soul, your gifts, and your higher purpose, as this chapter suggests.

Reevaluating the Company You Keep

When I was growing up, my mother used to say to me and my sister, Rose Marie, "You're judged by the company you keep—and the company you don't keep!" Looking back, I now realize what my mother was saying to us. Even when we are children, the friends we choose to associate with say something about us personally. Our friends somehow tell the world more about us, about our self-esteem, and about our personal interests.

> "No one can make you feel inferior without your consent." —ELEANOR ROOSEVELT

As I grew older, I began to see even more profoundly what keeping good company was all about. And I am not referring to people's social status, financial wealth, or physical attractiveness. Can you make the following declaration?

My Personal Declaration about the Company I Keep

My inner circle of friends speaks volumes about the kind of person I am. The people closest to me at this stage of my life reflect my level of confidence and self-worth; they make me want to stretch myself and do better every day. The company I keep strengthens my ability to flex every muscle of talent that I possess. My friends expect me to live my higher truth and to know my greater purpose and pursue it with unwavering determination. The company I keep acknowledges the unlimited possibilities within me.

My friends exemplify the criteria I've set for the kind of people with whom I choose to spend my time.

So how do you set the criteria for the people you let into your life? I know that an important criterion for me in any friendship is loyalty. I don't just mean being loyal when it's comfortable or convenient. I am referring to fierce loyalty, extreme loyalty, fanatical loyalty. The kind of loyalty that puts people by your side even when you're not riding high on success. The kind of loyalty that has your friends standing up for you when you need them most—when you're not around to defend yourself. For me, the loyalty my friends and I have to one another is the glue that binds us through thick and thin. If you can't commit to this level of loyalty, I probably won't be counting you among the friends I keep.

It's your life. Therefore, you, and you alone, set the criteria for the company you choose to keep. Here is one way to get clear on your personal criteria and to determine up front the characteristics of friendship that are most important to you.

NAVIGATION TOOL: *Establishing Criteria for Your Inner Circle of Influencers*

Now is a good time to stop and consider the criteria you will set for your inner circle of support and motivation. Make a list of those criteria. For example, I just shared with you one of my nonnegotiable criteria—extreme loyalty. What are your nonnegotiable criteria for the people you will count among your best friends and advisers? It's not okay to settle for less, but it is okay to expect more.

To get you started, here are a few examples of what you might consider listing.

The Company I Keep Will Be Made Up of Individuals Who Are...

- Fiercely loyal
- Faithful and trustworthy
- Tolerant of people's differences
- Generous with their ideas and innovations
- Secure about themselves and where they are going
- Positive and focused
- Intelligent and accomplished
- Family oriented

➤ Forgiving

➤ Building their lives from the inside out

➤ Now add your criteria here.

The Company I Keep Will Be Made Up of Individuals Who Are...

➤ _____

➤ _____

➤ _____

➤ _____

➤ _____

➤ _____

This is an important exercise. You'll soon find out that on the journey to living your fullest life, there is no room for people who cannot accept your higher truth and largest dreams. None. You are entitled to your passion and your dreams, and you have every right to believe in them fully and to have the kind of people around you who support your quest unconditionally. Never put yourself in a position where you have to defend your desires or convince others to accept your way of thinking. That's not what discovering True North is about. It's better to have 10 real friendships than 1000 apparent friends. Needless to say, you may find that your list of real friends is quite small, but that they are very powerful and influential in your life and your quest for your True North.

NAVIGATION TOOL: *Selecting the Company You Will Keep and the Company You Won't Keep*

Now that you've taken the time to identify the criteria by which you will reevaluate and select the company that you intend to keep, continue the process by listing specific individuals here. Write down their names. Then make a list of the people you may want to avoid. These are the people who consistently make you feel small and insignificant.

Those with Whom I'd Like to Keep Company

➤ _____

➤ _____

➤ _____

Those Whom I'm Better Off Avoiding

➤ _____

➤ _____

➤ _____

This is not a numbers game. You're not judged by the number of people that you associate with. You may, however, be judged by the company that you keep.

How You See Yourself and the Pitfalls of Contradicting Behaviors

You already have within you a deep sense of who you are and what you are about. Way down deep, there is a crystal-clear explanation of why you want to achieve certain things in this life or to strive to make the world a better place—living your best life, and reaching for your highest potential. But the only way this greater potential can rise up from your soul is if you are true to yourself in every way. This requires surrounding yourself with people who not only support you but allow you to be accountable to that higher truth and objective without compromise. And remember, if you're going to compromise, compromise up!

You cannot live your best life and perform at your highest level if the people with whom you surround yourself are behaving in a manner that is inconsistent with the way you see yourself. What I mean by this is that if you are saying that you want to make the most of yourself and go for the gold ring, but you are spending your time with people who behave in ways that are contradict your values, or who couldn't care less about how they make a difference and exhibit low levels of self-worth, or who live life ridiculing others for trying to be their best—then the company you're keeping is certain to sabotage your every effort to find your True North.

Many plans for a greater life have quickly evaporated simply because someone allowed the wrong people to surround him or her for too long, get too close, and influence his or her ideas and dreams in a negative way. Your greater potential can easily fall victim to the negative influence of those who don't, or can't, dwell in the greater possibilities that life has to offer. Some people are just unsympathetic and overly judgmental. Surprisingly, these people often really do care about us and love us. But they may be ill equipped to be part of our cheering gallery and our greater system of support and encouragement. Their ongoing disapproval, lack of compassion and understanding, need to discourage others, and never-ending warnings about taking risks are nothing less than extremely disappointing and emotionally draining.

Why People Who Love Us Bring Us Down

After the first day of a 2-day workshop from my Human Potential seminar series, one young man told me that while he was doing the evening assignment from the workshop, his father actually harassed him about the course and ridiculed the very idea of his discovering True North at all.

I wondered why the young man wanted to share his pursuit with his father at all, knowing full well that he'd be opening himself up to criticism and mockery. His response was that because he was enthusiastic about the program, he assumed that his father would be enthusiastic for him. Instead, what he got was an evening of letdown and dismay.

I explained that his father's reaction probably had nothing to do with how much he loved his son, but rather had more to do with his father's feeling threatened by his son's inner discovery and dreams for a greater future—dreams that might one day take him away from the family. And because of his own fear of change, risk, and failure, his father may have genuinely believed that such a course was going to inevitably be destructive to his son.

The young man's experience with his father was not an unusual one. The reality is that our closest friends, family members, husbands, wives, and other life partners often fear that if the person they care about most pursues a greater life, that person will change, and she or he may leave them for higher ground, smarter work, or a better life with more supportive friends. They may also fear that any drastic changes that their loved one makes will drastically change the relationship as well. If this is a concern in your life, here are some things you can do.

The Incubation Stage

As the higher purpose statement at the beginning of this chapter states, be true to the wisdom of your highest inner counsel. In other words, sometimes you have to keep your thoughts to yourself. At the beginning of your journey, seek your own inner counsel of guidance and advice. Unless you feel extremely confident that the person with whom you are about to share your life's dreams and goals will support your quest 110 percent, will be there to cheer you on through the entire journey, and will believe in you as much as you do, then stop and reconsider discussing your plan with that person.

In the beginning, keeping your larger vision private until you feel more confident that you can recognize those who will gleefully support you can save you an enormous amount of time spent explaining and defending yourself to those who simply don't get it. This is a waste of time to begin with. Either people get it or they don't. And if they don't, there's no sense in divulging your grand plan to them. You have a right to your privacy, and you have a right to your beliefs. Let this be the incubation stage of your personal growth until you have the right team and circle of friends in place. I'll discuss this in more detail and how to start putting into place a life board of directors later in this chapter.

Gravitate toward Like-Minded People

Next, seek out and gravitate toward like-minded people and people who are doing things in a greater, more successful way than you are doing them. People who share your belief in making quantum life changes and taking leaps of faith to pursue a better, fuller, more meaningful life are the kind of people that you need in your corner.

You should gravitate toward like-minded people—people who share similar beliefs and principles, and people with whom you have something in common. That doesn't mean people who will always agree with you. In fact, some of the best life coaches are those who can play devil's advocate and get you to examine all sides of a life challenge. These are people who have a vision of their own and are not complacent about going after their dreams full force. They may have already taken the journey and have reached their summit. Or they may be on a path similar to the one you are on right now. The point is to start actively seeking out individuals whom you admire. Align yourself with men and women who set the example for what you one day hope to achieve—those who have an appreciation for revealing life's greater possibilities with a plan of action and the perseverance to get there.

Doing this doesn't mean that you have to paint yourself into a corner and seek out only those people whom you can reach in person, people who are located in or near your own town or city. You don't even have to know these people. Why not gravitate toward people whom you've never met and may never meet in your lifetime? They can be even more influential in your quest by their sheer example. Since I would never suggest that you try something that I myself haven't tried and found effective, I'll share with you some life-changing techniques that I used when I was taking my own leap of faith.

Taking the Leap of Faith

After 17 years of working in the television and public relations industry, to people on the outside looking in, I appeared to have the best job in the world. I often went on media junkets where I got to hobnob with movie stars, political figures, and sports celebrities. Because of the media connection, I got to attend prestigious awards shows, celebrity-packed fund-raising galas, and even a few inaugural balls. Was it fun for a time? Yes. Was it my bigger dream, my inner passion, and my belief that I had become all that I could be? Absolutely not! But if I'd told anyone this at the time, that person would have said, "Are you crazy? You have the dream job of a lifetime. Don't rock the boat!" However, I come from a long line of boat rockers, and, the truth be told, after the initial glitz and glamour wore off, the work became a daily grind and, for me, very unfulfilling.

Hollywood was interesting but unreal. I knew I had more to give. I wanted to do work that called on my higher intelligence and writing talents. I wanted more, even if everyone else thought I had it all. And later, when I landed my own morning talk show, I always had the nagging feeling in the back of my mind that I was meant to do something more meaningful with my life than go on press junkets and interview the next pop teen idol. However, this didn't stop me from acting in contradiction to my inner voice of wisdom. So against my better judgment, I continued to build my PR and training business—I was even named businesswoman of the year—and soon became tangled in all of the trappings of bigger and bigger business deals, including a public offering of my company's stock. It was this move, which never "felt" right to begin with, that eventually sucked all the life and resources out of me, my partner, and the company.

You may find this hard to believe, but looking back, it was all a blessing. You see, I needed to have the doors blown off my world to be able to take the leap of faith that was to eventually alter my life, in the best possible way, forever, leading me to my higher purpose and true calling.

After a good deal of soul searching and using the exercises and practices I have fine-tuned for you in this book, I knew exactly what I wanted to do. I'd found my True North, and I was going to move toward it, no matter what or how. More than anything, I wanted to write books and become a professional speaker and trainer. I had a burning passion to travel the world and help change people's lives for the better. I somehow knew deep inside that I could help change the face of corporate training by introducing programs that had substance and soul—programs and seminars that would inspire employees who had become complacent and unmotivated to perform at their highest levels and get fired up enough to stand for something in the process.

I spent the next 4 years, while still working in PR and corporate training, developing myself as a writer and speaker and preparing myself for the ultimate leap of faith. This was my passion, and I was going to use every ounce of my being to make it happen. This doesn't mean that I didn't make all the typical blunders. I even mentioned to the wrong people that I wanted to change careers and make my living writing books and speaking around the world. You can probably guess their reaction: "Well, how do you expect to do that?" "There's no security in that kind of work." "Do you know how difficult it will be to get a publishing house to publish your book?" "What will you do for a real job?" And even when they weren't saying it out loud, they were thinking, "Who do you think you are?" But I wasn't about to let the naysayers lessen me, as I'd done so often in the past. I was ready to magnify my soul's intentions, use my gifts to write and speak publicly, and concentrate on my higher purpose. I realized at that moment that if you really want to get fired up about your passion, you have to set yourself on fire!

I did this by investing in myself. I attended professional speakers' conferences all over the country and paid full fare to watch the best of the best public presenters in the world do their thing. I took notes; I bought their books, watched their videos, and studied their web sites. I contacted speakers' bureaus from New York to Tucson inquiring about what it took to get on board. Then I bought every book I could find on how to get published, how to write a book proposal, and how to write a best-seller.

But one of the most important things I did was this: I gravitated toward people who were doing what I wanted to do in the public-speaking arena and the publishing world. These were people who weren't just doing it well, but were doing it extraordinarily well, exceptionally well, and I was their student, absorbing every bit of advice and every bit of inner wisdom that anyone would share with me. I called speakers and authors and interviewed them over the telephone, but there were also those whom I studied from afar.

I said earlier that you should gravitate not only toward like-minded people, but also toward people greater than yourself, people who are more successful than you are at this moment. What I mean by this is that you should start studying the people who are living their dream—people who are applying their extraordinary inner wisdom and unshakable faith to what they do. Seek out people who you think are living their higher truth and greatest potential. Then make a connection. Read about them, watch their videotapes and CDs, find out what their personal philosophies are and how they practice those philosophies, investigate how they overcame adversity, and look for what drives them toward a greater purpose.

Meeting these dynamic speakers and authors in person was never my goal—the goal was to gravitate toward them in whatever way I could because they were doing what I hoped one day to do for a living. If I got lucky and met someone along the way, that was icing on the cake. But typically, that wasn't the case.

For example, when I found out that Stephen King had written a book on how to become a successful author, I bought it. I'd never read even one Stephen King novel, but I had always been impressed with the way he got his career as a writer going and the solid relationships he had built within both the publishing world and the entertainment industry. I set out to gravitate toward Stephen King, but I've never met him and probably never will.

Did he influence me to want to write a novel and a screenplay one day? Yes. His book *On Writing* is one of the finest, if not the finest, no-nonsense, practical books on how to become a successful writer that I have ever read. As writers go, I consider Stephen King greater and more successful than myself. So, Mr. King, if you're reading this, I've added you to my life board of directors.

Create a Life Board of Directors

One of the strategies that you, too, can implement that will help you to magnify your soul, your gifts, and your higher purpose is to create what I call a life board of directors.

Think about it. Companies large and small spend a good deal of time and money courting just the right people and inviting those people to become members of the board of directors. Not only is this considered a prestigious position, but it also conjures up the image of people who are at the helm of an organization, steering its course toward greater success and future growth. It seems appropriate that we use the same approach in our personal lives as well.

As you begin your journey to realizing your greater potential, wouldn't it be nice to have your own life board of directors that you can turn to and call on for guidance, wisdom, and experience along the way? I have had a life board of directors in place for several years now, and it has continued to serve me as a source of ongoing support, inspiration, and higher learning. It is my suggestion that you set up such a board right away. And here is how to do it.

My Life Board of Directors Exercise

You are the chairperson of the board. Imagine yourself sitting at the head of the table (see Figure 2-1). Who are the board members who will be sitting with you? You will soon be writing in the names of the board members around the table. These people will play key roles in influencing your journey to a higher purpose and more gratifying life. You may know some of these people, and there may be others whom you do not know. We'll come back to this part later. First, take a moment to complete the following exercise.

NAVIGATION TOOL: *Determining Who Will Sit on Your Life Board of Directors*

Here are some questions that will help you in selecting your life board of directors. Remember that these people will assist you in moving forward on your journey to discover True North. Their support of your efforts and their own life examples, both personal and professional, should be your criteria for deciding whom you choose to put on your board.

Respond to the following:

- ➤ With whom do you feel absolutely safe? Whom can you trust?

- ➤ Whom can you rely on for the hard truth when it's required?

- ➤ Whom can you count on for inspiration and honest advice?

- ➤ Who's always been in your cheering gallery? Who never fails to lend you support?

➤ Who would be an exceptional industry-specific expert to advise you as you pursue your lifelong passion? (Name someone from a specific career area, i.e., a professor, doctor, writer, artist, management consultant, musician, aviation expert, travel writer, movie star, singer, stand-up comedian, real-estate developer, marketing analyst, politician, and so on.)

➤ Who would make an exceptional financial adviser?

➤ Who can help you to keep a better life balance between work and home?

➤ Whom would you most like to have take on the role of spiritual counselor?

➤ Who would make an enthusiastic health and fitness coach?

➤ Whom do you know that can help you plan your higher education or advanced degree program?

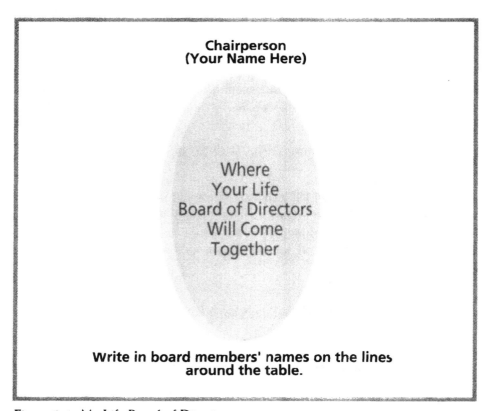

Figure 2-1. My Life Board of Directors

Now you can add your own customized questions to the list, questions that will best suit your specific needs.

The responses you give will help reveal to you the names of the people who are most qualified to sit on your life board of directors—those who are most in alignment with your goals. This board will become your inner circle of support. There may only be five or six people on your board, or there may be a dozen or more. Quality is what's important here, not quantity.

Now go back to the beginning of this exercise and write the names of your board members around the table. After you do this, take a separate sheet of paper and write the board members' names on it. Under each name, write why you have selected this person and what you expect to gain from this person's influence:

EXAMPLE:

My Board Member's Name

➤ _____

Why I Have Selected This Person

➤ _____

➤ _____

➤ _____

What I Expect

➤ _____

➤ _____

➤ _____

As time goes on and your journey continues to evolve, you may find different, even more appropriate board members. Make it a goal to not have any one person sit on your board for more than 2 years. This will encourage you to continually seek new inspiration and guidance and to rotate board members who can contribute the most appropriate input at the most appropriate time. Someone who is a valued contributor to your life board of directors today may not be the best adviser for you 2 years from now.

By keeping your board fresh and keep it moving forward, you will be cultivating people in your life who will generously feed your mind, body, and soul.

3

Self-Esteem Is Intelligence in Action

Higher Purpose Statement

Use all forms of your intelligence—intellectual, emotional, spiritual, and so on—to shape your choices and apply your natural gifts and competencies. The power of your self-perception is mightier than, and can overcome, any damage done to your self-confidence during your childhood or other life experiences that may have brought you down. Avoid the drama that often travels the low road of self-esteem and keep moving toward the high road. Carry yourself with pride. Walk and talk with confidence and self-assurance. Accord yourself kindness, generosity, and self-respect at all times.

Feeling Good about Yourself Is a Choice

No one can talk you into feeling good about yourself. That is a choice that only you can make. And every choice you make requires you to activate your mind and your intellect. Hence, self-esteem is intelligence in action, not an accidental discovery. But here's the key: Don't assume that when I use the word *intelligence*, I am simply referring to a person's IQ. I am not—in fact, far from it. There are several kinds of human intelligence, and, when they are combined and activated, they can help us reach our greater potential and implement our core competencies. I am referring to such forms of intelligence as spiritual intelligence, social skills intelligence, and emotional intelligence, or what used to be commonly called EQ (emotional quotient) but is now called EI (emotional intelligence).

All of Our Intelligences Play a Role in Creating Our Self-Esteem

Human intelligence: Intelligence is one of our most basic senses; it is described as the capacity to solve problems and meet challenges.

Intelligence Quotient (IQ): This is a ranking or number that denotes a person's intelligence relative to the average. The average IQ in the United States has risen, and there has been a similar increase in developed countries worldwide, primarily as a result of better nutrition, children completing more schooling, computers, and smaller family sizes.

Emotional intelligence (EI): EI is made up of human "soft" skills and competencies, such as self-confidence, integrity, and listening. Emotional intelligence refers to the capacity for recognizing our own feelings and those of others, motivating ourselves, and managing emotions in ourselves and in our relationships.

Spiritual intelligence: This is the ability to reach higher levels of consciousness and to find soulfulness and greater purpose through a higher power or divine force: God, Buddha, the Spirit, and so on.

Social skills intelligence: This is the ability to understand, interact with, and relate to people, and to act wisely in human relationships.

Interpersonal intelligence: This is the ability to understand people's needs, work cooperatively with others, and be competent in managing relationships and leading teams.

Intrapersonal intelligence: This involves possessing a higher level of self-awareness, self-actualization, and empathy.

In his best-selling book *Working with Emotional Intelligence,* Daniel Goleman refers to a person's strong sense of self-worth and self-confidence as an important life competence that is part of emotional intelligence (see the exercise in Chapter 5 on the power of human competencies). Goleman says that people with this competence have the strength to make tough decisions and to follow a specific course of action. He also points out that self-confident individuals are decisive without being arrogant or defensive, stand up for their decisions and choices, and can voice views that are unpopular, often going out on a limb for what they believe is right.

And so it's important for you to recognize the different shapes and appearances of your human intelligence and what that intelligence looks like in action when it is applied to the ups and downs of your self-esteem during your lifetime.

Renegotiating Self-Worth

Throughout your lifetime, your self-esteem is likely to fluctuate greatly. There are times when you are smarter than you are at other times. There are occasions when you have been a kinder person than you were at other times. And at certain periods in your life, you may not have been particularly deserving of high self-esteem because of your behavior and your treatment of others. My point is this: We continually renegotiate our sense of self-worth at various stages and ages of our life. And as we do this, we are making critical choices regarding the way we perceive ourselves. Whether those choices are good or bad, right or wrong, they are the choices that we are making at that moment in time. The choice may begin in your heart or in your gut, but it is in your brain that your own brand of intelligence in action is activated.

Whether you call it self-esteem, self-confidence, self-assurance, or self-acceptance, your self-regard is in your hands, and in your hands alone. The important choices you make that shape your life will contribute directly to either positive or negative self-esteem. Those choices can empower and energize you, or they can render you helpless and self-defeating. It's the force behind the choices we make that gives us the confidence to feel worthy and deserving of greater happiness.

Throughout life, we make certain choices that help us to build the resilience that enables us to cope with life's challenges and to build the entitlement that we use to assert our deepest needs and enjoy our greatest rewards and successes. When we fall down and injure our self-worth, it is the choices that we make from that point forward that give us the ultimate power from within to pick ourselves up and keep moving forward.

Our intellect helps us choose whether we will take the high road or the low road when it comes to self-esteem.

Case Study

This case study is a real-life story of two sisters—one who chose the low road of self-esteem and self-worth and one who chose the high road. This story has been adapted from a Building Self-Esteem seminar that I conducted a few years ago in Dallas, Texas.

Two Sisters: One Takes the High Road and One Takes the Low Road of Self-Esteem

Margaret's Story

Margaret is 36 years old. Her self-esteem is, and always has been, extremely low. Margaret says that her low self-worth has been pounded into her all her life and that she just can't shake it. She has one sister, named Jennifer. The sisters are 2 years apart in age, and Margaret is the younger. Both of them grew up in a very negative and demeaning environment. "Both our mother and our father never hesitated to tell us girls how 'pitiful and worthless' we were," says Margaret. "We were never allowed to shine. Every time we reached the smallest accomplishment, our parents would squash the possibility of experiencing any pride or self-worth whatsoever."

Margaret is now married and has three children of her own. "Although I have cut all ties with my parents, I cannot shake my low self-esteem no matter how hard I try," she says. "I continue to feel worthless and stupid, and I am fearful that this self-loathing is going to haunt me for the rest of my life. How do I create a higher self-worth for myself? I don't want my children to grow up seeing my low self-esteem as an example of how to live." Margaret has taken the low road of self-esteem.

Jennifer's Story

An interesting part of this scenario is that Margaret's older sister, Jennifer, does not suffer from low self-esteem. In fact, Jennifer exhibits a very healthy and positive self-image and exudes a great deal of self-confidence. Jennifer has a thriving business in New York City and presents herself with assurance and competence, both at home and on the job. Unlike Margaret, Jennifer stands up to life's challenges with gusto and goes after what she wants, making choices that get her where she wants to go. Jennifer obviously believes in herself and has a high level of self-esteem. Jennifer has chosen the high road of self-esteem.

How can two sisters, both of whom were raised in the same negative and degrading environment, be on such opposite sides of the self-esteem scale? It's easy. Each made life choices based on her own self-perception. First, let's look at Margaret's situation.

Margaret's story, sadly, is a common one. There is no doubt that her self-image was greatly damaged by the two main authority figures in her life—her own parents. Their unrelenting criticisms and cruelty wounded her self-confidence and self-image dramatically. But that's over, and Margaret can do something about her self-image. The real tragedy here is that up to this point, Margaret has willfully "chosen" to take over her parents' role of abuse by continuing to assault herself in their absence, forgetting that her hurtful upbringing in fact ended years ago.

By repeating the destructive cycle that her parents started, Margaret actually chose to continue the work for them. Even as an adult, Margaret continues to hold on to the perception of herself as a child, when what she actually needs is to let it go and create a new and stronger perception of herself today as a woman, wife, and mother.

Pivotal Point

No matter what your background or upbringing, your interaction with others, or your life experiences, in the final calculation, your self-worth is entirely in your hands. And in this scenario, Margaret has yet to realize the enormous power that she holds.

The message is this: You, and you alone, have complete control and power over how you perceive yourself, and that power is more magnificent than any destructive mantras you may have been exposed to in the past.

Two Rules of Self-Esteem:

1. Your level of self-esteem is completely up to you.

2. There are no other rules.

The Power of Perception—It Raises Us Up or Tears Us Down

Despite the years she spent in the hands of ignorant parents, the influence and power that Margaret has over her own self-perception are far more powerful, and they also are exponential, whether they are used for positive or negative image building.

For example, up to this point, Margaret has used her power of self-perception in a negative way, and this has led to an exponential spiral further downward. By choice, she's continued to have negative conversations with herself and to apply negative labels to herself, such as calling herself stupid or unworthy. Margaret will never stop the downward spiral of her self-esteem if she continues the cycle of self-flagellation, self-criticism, and self-pity.

Margaret has not been putting all of her intelligence into action, and, as a result, she has taken the path of least resistance and lower self-worth.

The Power of Positive Reinforcement and Self-Talk

Just as negative self-talk can impede a person's fight for a better life, positive self-talk and positive reinforcement can instill in someone the will to go on and live abundantly.

> Don't you say your good-byes. Not yet. Do you understand me? Listen, Rose, you're gonna get out of here. You're gonna go on and you're gonna make lots of babies and you're gonna watch them grow. You're gonna die an old lady warm in her bed. Not here. Not this night. Not like this. Do you understand me?
> —Jack to Rose, clinging to a piece of debris in the north Atlantic Ocean, from the movie *Titanic*

The Transformation

It was in this seminar, one hot summer day in Dallas, that I watched Margaret's self-perception literally be transformed.

After Margaret shared her story, the group asked her one simple and straightforward question. The group members asked her to take a look at what her sister, Jennifer, had been doing differently all these years, even though Jennifer had been raised in the very same negative environment. Margaret was then asked to make a list of the things that demonstrated her sister's "intelligence in action"—all those things that put her sister on the high road of self-confidence and self-assurance. During that interactive exercise, several key issues rose to the surface, clearly distinguishing the differences in the actions taken and choices made by the two sisters. And with this exercise a great life transformation took place for Margaret.

> "I was brought up to believe that how I saw myself was more important than how others saw me."
> —ANWAR EL-SADAT, FORMER EGYPTIAN PRESIDENT

Author's Note: For the purpose of this book, and in order to get to the point of each issue quickly in the limited space available in this chapter, I have summarized some of the critical choices and actions that Margaret believed her sister Jennifer had taken to reach the high road of self-esteem.

According to Margaret, Jennifer's intelligence in action included, but was not limited to, the following:

➤ As an adult, Jennifer made a conscious choice not to believe what her parents had hammered into her all those years. She was able to separate her emotional feelings of hurt and disappointment from her intellect and from her self-perception, or the kind of person she knew herself to be deep down. She discovered that she could overpower her parents' actions with her own intellect and independent thinking. She put her various intelligences (IQ, emotional, spiritual, social, and so on) into action to create ongoing self-affirmation, eventually drowning out the messages of negativity and shame.

➤ Jennifer believes that just being born makes her worthy to be here and to feel good about herself.

➤ Jennifer surrounds herself with people who feed her soul and create positive influences in her life.

➤ Jennifer believes that holding anyone else accountable for her happiness and self-worth is just a waste of time and that she alone is responsible for her happiness.

➤ She fully understands that not having gotten the love she deserved as a child isn't her fault, but that now it is entirely her responsibility to give herself the love she never received and to hold herself accountable for doing so.

➤ Jennifer knows that she has the power to change or enhance her self-perception and that by activating her brain and all of her intelligence, she can pave her own road—a high road of positive self-worth—and move forward full steam ahead.

After completing this list, Margaret shared her thoughts and the list with her seminar teammates. They had her compare her own actions and choices with the actions and choices of her sister. The gap was evident, and so were the reasons why. Using this exercise as a life compass, Margaret slowly began the process of taking full responsibility for how she treated herself and the self-perception that she held.

"Things do not change; we change."
—HENRY DAVID THOREAU

LIFE COMPASS: *Are You Choosing the High Road or the Low Road of Self-Esteem?*

Here is your chance to activate your inner guidance system and start developing higher self-esteem by completing this Life Compass exercise. Be sure to give yourself enough time to answer and respond to each of the following questions.

1. Do your actions and decisions diminish or increase you as a person? In what ways?

2. How do you carry yourself? Do you resonate a high-road or low-road presence? Do you walk with confidence? Do you speak with confidence? Do you voice your opinions? If not, why not?

3. Do you possess authentic pride in your actions and behaviors? In what ways?

4. Do you find it easy to speak of your accomplishments when you are asked about them? If not, why not?

5. Do you take comfort in giving compliments to and receiving them from others? Or do you cringe when someone showers you with praise?

6. Are you genuinely happy for other people's good fortune, or do you secretly feel jealous and angry?

7. Are you overly sensitive, or do you laugh at yourself with ease and enjoy the humorous aspects of life?

8. Describe your body language. Do you cross your arms and appear defensive when someone approaches you for discussion, or are your body language and tone of voice open and welcoming?

9. Do you feel worthy of having good things happen in your life? Do you attract good things to you, or do you attract negativity and crisis?

10. Do you accord yourself generosity and self-respect? If yes, explain. If not, why not?

Your responses to the questions in this Life Compass exercise will help you to quickly detect whether you are traveling on the high road of self-esteem and moving closer to your True North, or whether you are traveling on the low road of self-esteem and perpetuating an already low self-image and inaccurate self-perception. If you're traveling the high road most of the time, then you are doing just fine. However, if you are traveling the low road more often than you'd like, it's time for you to find out why and do something about it. Only you can make this happen. Knowing what you have learned up to this point eliminates all of your excuses not to try.

The High Road Is Sometimes a Radical Path of Risk and Fear

If you're not traveling the high road of self-esteem, it's time for you to find out why. For starters, you already know that you cannot use your past experiences as an excuse not to travel to higher ground. Only you can transform your life and change what you believe about yourself. This brings us to a key observation: Wherever you stand, right here, right now, in life, it is your own beliefs about yourself—your self-perception—and no one else's that put you there. So what are you willing to do about it?

The high road of self-esteem is often paved with things that scare us, like taking risks. According to the highly acclaimed work of David K. Reynolds, who studies and teaches "lifeway" and gives training courses called Constructive Living, one of the reasons that people who lack self-esteem do so is because they haven't taken enough risks, which might lead them to greater successes. His practices come from Japanese therapies called Morita and Naikan. In the Morita therapy, the precept is: Be scared to death and do what you have to do. In other words, you can practice countless techniques for raising your self-worth, from visualizing your success to reciting affirmations, day and night, but without action in the face of what you fear, you will only be anesthetized or distracted from what you actually need to be doing in order to experience the fear, the risk, and ultimately the success.

This principle seems to be in sharp contrast to what we practice in our American culture, where the drive for success comes first, followed by the need to feel good about ourselves, or just to feel good all the time, period. For example, why feel anxiety, when you can take a pill? Why be tense or nervous? There's a pill for that, too. The principle of Dr. Reynolds's teachings is that it's okay to feel anxiety, to feel sadness, or to worry because feeling these emotions is what drives people to take action, experience their fears, and then do something about those fears.

Fear—The Great Immobilizer

It is through taking bold actions in the face of fear that you will move toward your higher purpose and the grander vision that the universe holds for you. Fear can and will completely immobilize you if you let it, and it can keep you from becoming your best self and living your best life. So whatever you fear most, know this: It has absolutely no power over you—none, zip, zero. What *does* have tremendous and debilitating power is the actual fear that you are feeling within you. Whatever the *thing* that you fear may be, it, alone, cannot touch you or affect you. But once you allow fear to enter your mind, it will be insidious. Not only will it take over your thoughts, but it will start robbing you of your life, a piece at a time. This happens every time you give up a small part of yourself to your fear. By doing this, you relinquish your inner strength to the very thing you fear the most.

> "Anxiety seems to be the dominant fact—and is threatening to become the dominant cliché—of modern life."—*TIME* MAGAZINE

So is there a cure for fear? Yes. It's called courage. When you perceive yourself as being courageous in the face of fear, you will persevere, placing one foot in front of the other, pushing past your anxiety, and moving toward your True North.

I'll share an example. I have a good friend who is deathly afraid of flying. However, he must fly because his job requires him to travel all over the world. Sure, he could say, "I can't fly because I am deathly afraid of flying, and so I will have to miss that meeting in Amsterdam." But that would be a lie, because he can fly and be scared to fly, all at the same time. Facing his fear of flying head on does not require him to be completely comfortable with being on an airplane. It requires only that he do three things each time he must travel: buy a ticket, go to the airport, and board the flight. By shoring up the courage to put one foot in front of the other, my friend faces his fears, takes the risk, and then feels good about himself for not having given in to the panic or having given away a piece of his strength to the very thing he fears most.

> "The only thing we have to fear is fear itself."
> —FRANKLIN D. ROOSEVELT

I'm not saying this is easy. It is not. Whenever you muster the courage not just to step outside the box, but to actually blow up the box, the results may not always be pleasant, and you may actually want to quit, but the alternatives are much more frightening. If you give in to your fears and avoid taking risks, you may one day wake up and find yourself in a horrible rut—or, worse, you may wind up languishing in regret, wondering what life could have been like if you hadn't been so scared.

Is Your Search for Happiness and Self-Esteem a Drama That You Enjoy Living?

This is the last chapter in this week's lesson. And so here's my million-dollar question to you: Are you really willing to do what it takes to magnify your soul's higher purpose, or do you sometimes find yourself enjoying the drama of your life a little too much?

After years of facilitating workshops and seminars from my Human Potential Series, I have come to the conclusion that there are people out there who enjoy the drama of seeking, but who never really intend to find True North or to develop a healthy self-perception. Why? Because they simply don't want to make the effort that it takes to seriously alter their lives and change them for the better. After a while, what the heck, it's easier just to live the drama that keeps them stuck in negative patterns and habits than to put in the hard work that is necessary if they are to build a better life and to accept the fact that we are the only ones who have the power and ability to make any real change happen.

> "I have not the shadow of a doubt that any man or woman can achieve what I have, if he or she would make the same effort and cultivate the same hope and faith. What is faith worth if not translated into action?"
> —MOHANDAS GANDHI

It's all on our shoulders, and that hard-hitting message becomes too much for some people to acknowledge and accept, especially when it's far easier to simply blame others for our woes and point the finger at the people "who done me wrong." The reality is that for some people, it can be easier to sit in a psychotherapist's office and talk about why they can't change or why they can't heal the wounds of their past than it is to make the choice to take action and start doing what needs to be done—like my friend who faces his fear of flying and buys the plane ticket anyway.

Taking the high road works much the same way. How can you travel that road, or move toward True North, without some degree of fear? You can't. So how do you handle being faced with a risky or difficult decision about something? The answer is to remove fear from the equation. And the best way to do this is to start by asking yourself some basic questions, such as:

- ➤ What would I do in this situation if I could be myself and not care about making a mistake?

- ➤ How would I act if I weren't afraid my spouse would leave me and I'd be alone?

- ➤ What would I say if I wasn't afraid of appearing ignorant or foolish?

When you remove fear from the situation, an amazing thing happens—the answers you are seeking come sharply into focus, and so does your self-image.

EXERCISE

Try it. Practicing this process can transform your life. Think about something that holds you back and keeps you from moving forward to a higher path and a stronger self-image. Whatever it is that's holding you back, it's something that you believe about yourself. Change what you believe by addressing the issues and the fears you have. You can remove fear from the situation by asking yourself questions similar to the examples I've provided, and then taking action.

What I fear most/what's holding me back (write in your fears here):

_____

_____

NAVIGATION TOOL: *Write a Profile in Courage about Yourself*

Taking risks and building self-esteem is a learned behavior, not a gene that you inherit. Risk-taking behavior starts with baby steps that we build over time. More than likely, you have been taking risks all of your life, but not giving yourself credit for those risk-taking leaps of faith.

Here's an example. One of my clients wanted to start her own business out of her home so that she could have a more flexible work schedule and spend more time with her two children. The risk involved was that she would have to rely solely on herself to generate income and ongoing business development—a scary proposition for most folks.

My client was no different. She was completely terrified by the prospect of taking on the responsibilities of being self-employed. It was clear that she possessed all of the skills, education, and experience necessary to be successful, but she had a deeply rooted lack of self-confidence and fear of failure. Her self-talk was negative and unsupportive, as well. When we met, I let her know that before she could begin an entrepreneurial venture, she had to face her fears. I had her start by listing those fears and then posing these critical questions for each: What was the worst that could happen? If her venture failed, couldn't she, with her credentials, quickly land another job in journalism? How would she move forward if she had nothing to lose?

Next, I reminded her of all the risks she had successfully taken in the past. Her response was, "What risks?" In her mind, she had convinced herself that she had never demonstrated the courage and risk-taking mentality necessary to be her own boss. Here's how I convinced her that she was mistaken.

I asked my client to complete an exercise that I was certain would help build her self-confidence. I suggested that she write what I call a Profile in Courage about herself. The objective of this exercise is to resurrect the successful side of yourself—the side you so often bury and forget about. This process is likely to do two important things. (1) It reminds you of all the successes that you have had in the past, successes and accomplishments that you may have forgotten or that may have diminished in your mind over time. And since success and excellence are simply repeated efforts, once you have reminded yourself of your past accomplishments, both big and small, you begin getting yourself into a mindset that prepares you to take on bigger, more important endeavors. (2) You quickly come to recognize and appreciate your pattern of risk-taking behavior and how you have grown that competence over the years, starting with baby steps and moving on to bigger leaps of faith. For example, you may have started out with a one-bedroom starter home when you were 28 years old, but, over the years, you have gradually increased your purchases and financial responsibilities, and you now have a larger and higher-maintenance property.

By the time my client had completed her Profile in Courage, it was evident that she was fully prepared and competent to start this venture. In her profile, my client revealed that she had a long string of accomplishments to her name. Once she resurrected all of her successes, she was quickly reminded that she did have the perseverance, dedication, and intelligence to get the job done. In the process, she was actually transforming her self-esteem and confidence to a higher level.

The past successes that my client listed in her Profile in Courage included building an entire house with a Habitat for Humanity team, losing 12 pounds in a short period, learning and mastering classical piano, winning several journalism awards, earning a salary higher than she had ever dreamed she would make, getting a master's degree from Columbia, raising two self-confident, happy children, and syndicating one of her newspaper columns.

In an effort to address her concerns about her past risk-taking performance, I helped my client list many of the risks she had taken throughout her life, several of which she had turned into major life accomplishments. For example, she had never considered that taking out a student loan, which enabled her to go on to get her graduate degree in journalism, was in fact a risk. She just did it, and the risk paid off. She completed her degree and landed a prestigious reporting position at a highly respected newspaper in Washington, D.C. She has since paid off the loan. Two years later, she got married. I pointed out to her the risk she had taken in doing that, given that one in two marriages ends in divorce. She's been married for 18 years, and her marriage is a solid and happy one. I also pointed out to her that having two children was a risk, but she did it anyway, and that she and her husband have raised two bright and considerate kids. And even when the risks she took didn't pan out so well—like investing a big chunk of her portfolio in high-tech stocks right before the dot-com downturn—she in fact rebounded. Since that time, she's reevaluated her investment strategies and has bounced back in the market.

Now write your own Profile in Courage, detailing your life's successes and accomplishments and giving proper recognition to both the smaller and larger life risks you have undertaken. Whether or not they ended successfully isn't the issue. The fact that you took the risk is what is relevant to your ability to take more and greater risks in the future. Furthermore, you've already had accomplishments in the past, which is relevant to your future accomplishments and risk-taking abilities. Note that when risk is combined with vision, great things can result.

Bill Gates's Profile in Courage

When the risks we take are combined with our vision and our passion, great things can result. Many people thought that Bill Gates was foolish to drop out of Harvard in order to pursue a software business. But Gates had a singular focus and vision, which has revolutionized the way people all over the world live and do business. Gates today maintains the same vision for which he risked more than just a Harvard education: "A computer on every desk and in every home."

NAVIGATION TOOL: *My Profile in Courage*

In your Profile in Courage, describe the past accomplishments and successes of which you are most proud. Describe both personal and professional achievements. Next, detail the life risks you have taken and their outcomes. Can you detect a pattern in your behavior or actions when taking risks over the years? How have you graduated to taking more risks with greater comfort and confidence?

_____

_____

_____

_____

———————————————————————————

———————————————————————————

———————————————————————————

———————————————————————————

———————————————————————————

———————————————————————————

———————————————————————————

———————————————————————————

———————————————————————————

———————————————————————————

———————————————————————————

———————————————————————————

———————————————————————————

———————————————————————————

———————————————————————————

———————————————————————————

Now that you have completed your Profile in Courage, be sure to hold on to it, because you will use this document as an ongoing reference point and navigation tool that will assist you in determining where you've been and where you're going. Also, you will want to update it on an annual basis.

Self-Worth Requires Self-Work

By now, you've discovered from this chapter that nurturing your self-esteem and your self-image requires much more than just repeating selected mantras to yourself on a daily basis. Ultimately developing your self-worth requires self-work, and that means working to accord yourself the same respect, generosity, and consideration that you would give anyone else that you love. As you move closer to True North, you will begin defining the world in your own terms and making more and more intelligent choices. It is my hope that this week's lessons will help guide you in this process.

Moving into Your Equilibrium: Week 1 Review

Congratulations! You have completed the exercises in the chapters for Week 1 of the Discover True North program:

➤ If You're Going to Compromise, Compromise Up!

➤ Cultivate People Who Feed Your Soul—Create a Life Board of Directors

➤ Self-Esteem Is Intelligence in Action

Go back and review all three chapters' lessons and exercises and use the following four steps to reflect on what you learned in Week 1. Allow these four steps to help move you toward your equilibrium for higher learning and understanding. Think about how you have been able to improve your life using one section of this book at a time. How will you apply and practice each chapter's higher purpose statement in your own life?

STEP 1: *Stop and Breathe*

As you begin, clear your mind and reflect on the key points of Week 1 and what you've learned. Start by taking some deep breaths and slowly releasing them. Relax and consider how the lessons you have gleaned from these chapters might enhance or enlighten your life. Jot down ways in which you feel more confident or self-assured. Fully appreciate the new or higher perspectives that you may have gained from this week's lessons, which can lead you to the high road of self-esteem and confidence.

STEP 2: *Be Conscious and Think*

How has what you have learned this week served to raise your consciousness to a higher level? How will you benefit from your raised consciousness? List some of the ways in which you will activate your awareness levels. Write down what you know to be most important at this time and place in your life. How do you plan to maintain your focus and your attention to the details?

STEP 3: *Choose and Commit*

What life choices will you make and commit to carrying through after completing this week's lessons? In what ways do you anticipate that your choices will move you away from fear and closer to a newer, stronger inner wisdom? Give examples of how you will avoid taking a path of least resistance when you are faced with a challenge. What moments from this week's lessons represent your deepest truths? Describe the ways in which you demonstrate these truths on a daily basis.

STEP 4: *Act and Then Move toward Something*

How will you take action on what you've learned this week? List specific steps that you will take that will move you toward your higher purpose. How have the lessons this week guided you closer to your True North? What will you review and work on for ongoing improvement and personal development? What schedule will you set to accomplish this?

After completing these four steps, you are now ready to move on to Week 2, "No, You Can't Be Anything You Want, but You Can Be Anything You're Capable of Becoming."

WEEK

2

No, You Can't Be Anything You Want, but You Can Be Anything You're Capable of Becoming

4

Recognize and Activate Your Inner Voice of Wisdom and Courage

Higher Purpose Statement

To simply attain knowledge, you just have to keep adding to what you already know. But if you want to recognize and activate your inner voice of wisdom and courage, you need to let go of what you think you know so that you will start to understand your life's greater meaning and purpose. Know that your voice of inner wisdom will lend its guidance and direction to you long before your brain comprehends its message. When it has been fine-tuned, your inner voice will guide you in your quest for True North, revealing that the primary source of wisdom lies within and is as unique as the individual instruments that make up a symphony orchestra.

> "Each one of us has all the wisdom and knowledge we ever need right within us. It is available to us through our intuitive mind, which is our connection with universal intelligence."
> —SHAKTI GAWAIN, AUTHOR OF *DEVELOPING INTUITION AND CREATIVE VISUALIZATION*

Welcome to Week 2 in your journey to discover True North. This week's lessons are filled with blueprints of self-discovery. Each of them is an exploration into the truths and myths of our life's vocations and deeper callings, which I discuss in detail in Chapter 5. These lessons also provide an entrée to working in tandem with your own unique rhythms, cycles, and stages of life, as described in Chapter 6. However, our first subject in this week's program focuses on learning how to activate, or call forward, your inner voice of wisdom and courage—perhaps the most significant and sensitive Life Compass within your inner guidance system.

It still amazes me how easily our lives can be transformed when we open ourselves to guidance beyond the logical decisions we make. More than 100 years ago, Ralph Waldo Emerson wrote, "There is guidance for each of us, and by lowly listening we shall hear the right words." By carefully listening to and calling forward your higher intuition and innermost wisdom, you can quickly become aware of a greater guiding force, a force that you will be able to tune in to, hear more clearly, and respond to with greater faith and freedom of expression.

> "No more words. Hear only the voice within."
> —RUMI, POET

For clarification purposes, throughout this book, when I use the term *inner voice,* I will be referring to the source of greater wisdom and information that I believe lies within all of us. This inner voice is heard in the questions we ask ourselves, the answers we give, and the solutions to what we are seeking at any given time. This small, still voice is also known by many different names, including the voice of intuition, the Spirit, God, the Divine, and the higher self, to name a few. I personally like to think of my own inner voice as messages being played for me to the music of my life.

Your Inner Voice—The Music of Your Life

Life is more harmonious when we learn to sing and move to the rhythm of our inner voice. I believe that one of the ways in which we find our True North is by learning to recognize and activate our inner guidance system—a navigational system that is inherent in our humanity and is something we are born to use. When we

> Today I do affirm that I am Divinely guided. . . . There is that within which knows what to do and how to do it, and it compels me to act on what it knows.
> —ERNEST HOLMES

learn to place our faith in this intuitive guidance system, we discover that it will take us as far as we are willing to go. Your inner guidance system is composed of many Life Compasses, and, just as different instruments make up an orchestra, these compasses make up what I call the symphony of our lives. I think this is an appropriate metaphor because our inner voice has its own unique and distinct beat, rhythm, and melodious sounds. And when they are fine-tuned, these sounds gracefully guide us in our quest to be all that we can be in this lifetime. The primary source of wisdom lies within us and is as distinctive as the individual instruments that make up a symphony orchestra.

We live in a world that boasts of egalitarianism, which can sometimes make it difficult to hear and recognize our one-of-a-kind deeper voice of wisdom and greater purpose.

Simply put, your inner guidance system is the symphony orchestra that resides within you, and your inner voice is one of its instruments. Again, this metaphor works well to explain the importance of your own uniqueness, because an orchestra does not represent a hierarchy of instruments. Rather, an orchestra is made up of many instruments, all equally important but each unique in its own way. And like the instruments of your inner guidance system—one of which is your inner voice—each instrument in the symphony has its own sounds, without being better or more important than all the other instruments.

> "Music is your own experience, your thoughts, your wisdom. If you don't live it, it won't come out your horn."—CHARLIE PARKER, JAZZ MUSICIAN

You are the master musician of your individual instrument. And if you are to be able to play in life's symphony, it's good for you to be familiar with many of the other instruments out there, but you must first be the master of your own instrument. Every member of an orchestra is responsive to the unique sounds of his or her own instrument, allowing each individual note of music to emerge from the diversity of sounds around them, but never at the expense of its own individualism.

Discover Your Own Radical Uniqueness

Even though we are all players in the symphony of life, inseparable from one another in the universe, each of us can reach our destination, or our True North, only by listening to the music of our own instrument, our own inner voice, and that means that we all take a separate path on life's journey. You will never discover your True North if you don't exercise your character muscles of individuality and radical uniqueness. And that means trusting and placing your faith in that small, still voice within. In the words of Buddhist nun Ane Pema Chodron, "Faith will take you as far as you can go, and you'll understand all the teachings anyone has ever taught."

The Music Is Already in You, as Are the Answers You Seek

There is a famous story about the legendary violinist Niccolò Paganini and how he came upon his greatest truth and lesson in life.

One evening, as Paganini walked out on stage to perform before a sold-out opera house, the audience welcomed him with an overwhelming standing ovation. In those brief moments during the ovation, as he looked at his violin, Paganini realized that something wasn't right. He was not holding his violin. Instead, he had someone else's violin in his hands. He was horrified, and then he quickly composed himself, knowing that he had no choice at that moment but to play.

It is said that Paganini gave the performance of a lifetime that day. Afterwards, in his dressing room, Paganini spoke these words to a fellow musician: "Today, I learned the most important lesson of my entire career. Before today, I thought the music was in the violin; today I learned that the music is in me."

> "To better hear the world outside, listen faithfully to the voice inside."—QUAKER PROVERB

This story exquisitely portrays the unspoken inner talents and wisdom that lie deep inside each of us. The music of your life—your inner wisdom—is something that is already in you, just as the music was in Paganini. It is part of your overall inner guidance system, complete with a variety of life compasses to help you navigate to the tempo of your most authentic and unique self.

Self-Dialogue Activates Inner Wisdom

Dealing with our minds while trying to free up our ability to connect with our deeper self is an ongoing battle of life for most of us, and the battle is more difficult for some people than for others. After teaching hundreds of communications courses, I have excavated what I believe to be one of the simplest, yet most profound, navigation tools for activating your inner voice of wisdom. And in most cases, it all comes down to the way we ask questions—the self-dialogue about our lives that we engage in and the things we say that either move us forward or hold us back from being all that we are capable of becoming.

Asking Why Weakens Our Power to Move Forward

When you were a child, "Why?" was probably the question you used most when you were impatiently trying to get answers and to figure out just how the world works: "Why did Grandma die?" "Why do I have to eat my spinach?" "Why is the grass green?" But then we grow up, and somehow the "why" questions don't seem to work as effectively for us as they used to. One reason for this is that asking why often does little more than keep us stuck in our despair and weaken our power to move forward toward True North. For example, have you ever spent time asking yourself questions like these: "Why can't I be thinner?" "Why am I not prettier?" "Why can't I meet a nice guy like Linda's husband?" "Why do these things always happen to me?" "Why can't I ever do anything right?"

In my workshop Communications Excellence, one of the first things we learn is how to improve our self-dialogue so that we can gain wisdom from the questions we ask ourselves and others, and then use that wisdom to move us forward. I like to point out early in the session that asking "why" questions can quickly fill your mind with emotions and blame—or just a lot of generic information—but not a lot of wisdom.

Train Your Brain to Seek Wisdom, Not Just More Information

Our self-dialogue and the questions we ask in our life can be habit-forming. So how do you break the habit of asking "why" questions? You start by training your brain to call up your inner wisdom, not just more frustrating information that can keep you from achieving the answers you are seeking.

I like author and life coach Laura Berman Fortgang's approach. In her book *Living Your Best Life*, she suggests that you think of your brain as one big Yahoo! search engine. She says that thinking of your mind as a search engine is like tapping into a data bank of information that you already have available to you, made up of acquired experience, knowledge, and intuition. Fortgang, the president of InterCoach, Inc., goes on to say that by forming questions that serve as your key words, your brain searches its resources and gives you possible answers, and that the more specific your keyword entry, the more specific the answers—just as when you're on the Internet. Makes sense to me.

So how do you get to those questions that will unearth the answers from your inner wisdom and not just more useless data? How do you go about asking "smart" questions? One way is to start training your brain to ask "what" questions on a more regular basis. Believe me, the results can be both extraordinary and immediate. For example, when I facilitate a communications workshop, I start out by asking the group to write down the answer to this question: "Why are you here taking this course?" Almost everyone writes something about how the inability to communicate better has negatively affected his or her life or his or her relationships at home or on the job. The answers almost always focus on looking backward, bringing more problems and frustrations bubbling to the surface.

Next, I ask this question: "What do you hope to gain by attending this workshop?" All right, now we're cookin'! Inevitably this question forces everyone to look forward. People reply with things like, "To improve my relationship with my spouse and children," "To learn and implement better communications tools and techniques in my work," or "To live a better life because I will become a better communicator." See what I mean? Every answer to the "what" question is moving the person forward and in a positive direction, not backward and in a negative direction. Also, the answers to "what" questions are more specific and less cluttered than the answers we get from the "why" questions that we ask out of habit.

Your "what" questions can transform your life by releasing and activating a momentum of positive energy and moving you into a realm of possibility and higher inner wisdom. "What" questions are "smart" questions when it comes to developing new and more positive behaviors.

NAVIGATION TOOL: *Transforming "Why" Habits to "What" Behaviors*

During this week, I want you to practice using "what" questions to activate your inner voice of wisdom and to start breaking the habit of asking the "why" questions that are more than likely keeping you stuck.

Remember, by asking "what" questions, you will automatically be shifting the emphasis from simply gathering details of general information to achieving valuable outcomes and solutions, the answers provided by your inner voice of wisdom. Here are some examples to help you get started.

LIFE COMPASS: *Communication Toolkit*

The Transformation from "Why" Habits to "What" Behaviors Activates Your Inner Voice of Wisdom

PERSONAL "WHY" QUESTIONS NOT TO ASK	INNER WISDOM ACTIVATORS— "WHAT" QUESTIONS TO ASK
Why am I not better at this?	What can I do to improve my skills?
Why does she always get everything she wants?	What can I do to start getting the things I want?
Why do men always treat me badly?	What kind of men am I choosing to date?
Why am I always behind?	What can I do to move ahead?
Why don't my friends trust me?	What can I do to earn other people's trust?
Why don't I get included more often?	What can I do to get included?
Why do I need a degree for that job?	What can I do to get my degree?

Why do I always procrastinate?

What can I do make better decisions early on and not always wait until the last minute?

Why am I always late?

What can I do to prevent myself from always being late?

Why am I always broke?

What can I do to get out of debt?

Here's what I want you to do: During this entire week, start training your brain to practice asking your own "what" questions. Catch yourself every time you ask a "why" question that requires deeper answers and solutions, and then reframe that same question starting with "what."

Keep a log of the questions you are transforming and how they are helping you to activate your inner voice of wisdom and knowledge.

Turning Inner Wisdom into On-the-Job Performance

Like any communication tool, what you do to develop yourself on a personal level can often be used effectively in the workplace, and vice versa. For example, rather than asking an employee, "Why do you have such a bad attitude?" try asking, "What do you think we should do to remedy your dissatisfaction?" Or rather than asking, "Why are you sulking and being such a downer?" ask, "What would you like to see happen and what would you specifically do to make things better, given our resources?" The idea is to keep asking questions that will move the person to solution-seeking answers, not more complaining and whining. By doing this, you'll be accessing the other person's inner wisdom and knowledge—the information that person already knows deep down to be true and wise—and then giving the person an opportunity to reveal that wisdom.

One workshop student wrote me the following letter sharing with me his experience on the job and how he used what he learned to better handle a difficult employee situation.

Dear Ms. Bruce,

Shortly after taking your Communications Excellence program, I found myself in the perfect situation to utilize my Life Compass: Communications Toolkit.

While conducting a performance review for an employee, all of my recommendations and input were met with hostility and a negative attitude. My initial response, and what I would have done before attending your workshop, would have been to ask her, "Why do you always have such a bad attitude?" "Why do you think any of us would want to help you when you are so rude all the time?" "Why don't you stop complaining long enough to try to make a difference around here?" But I remembered what I had learned and stopped myself from asking all the tempting "why" questions I would have posed in the past.

Instead, I suggested that we take a short break. During that time, I composed my thoughts and reviewed the exercise I had completed in the course. A few minutes later, we reconvened. This time my approach was one of seeking solutions and moving this person forward in a positive manner. So I asked her, "Tell me what it is that you find so upsetting about your performance review." "You're obviously upset; what emotions has this discussion triggered for you?" "What goals would you like to set for yourself this year?" "What do you suggest we do to measure your success?" "What is it you want that will make you happy in your job?" "What can I do to help you be more successful?"

Instantly, I witnessed a transformation in this person. No longer was she able to wallow in the past and pull me down with her. And although she seemed flabbergasted by my "what" questions at first, she was now envisioning the future and slowly starting to describe what she wanted. Without realizing it, she was using her inner wisdom—she had all of the answers to her own gripes and grievances, and now she was accessing those answers and sharing them with me. Also, my "what" questions left no room for excuses, and I think she was completely bowled over by that alone, and so was I!

I never would have been able to reach this level of communication with this particular employee had I not put these techniques to use.

Thanks again,

Jim
Portland, Maine

At the end of this week's lesson, take time to record your experiences with this communications technique. What conversations seemed to go more smoothly? What did you learn about shifting the emphasis from just gathering information to gaining real answers and asking more meaningful questions? How do you feel about incorporating this technique into your life on a regular basis?

Activate Your Inner Voice of Courage

In addition to your inner voice of wisdom, which is always there to guide you, you also have an inner voice of courage and authentic bravery. I believe that the universe gives courage when we need it most.

EXERCISE: *My Most Courageous Moments*

Think about the instances in your life when you have faced difficult times or dangerous and demanding situations—the times when you rose to the occasion in a way you never thought you could, when all of a sudden, from out of nowhere, you seemed to have the power and strength to do the unimaginable. Many of us have experienced those moments in our lives.

Take time here to reflect on and document those instances. Be specific about the fear you felt and what it took to overcome that fear, move forward, and take action, pulling from within you every ounce of courage available.

My Most Courageous Moments Have Included the Following

_____

_____

_____

_____

Next, describe the results of bringing forth your inner courage. Whose lives were affected? What might have happened if you hadn't been there to take action?

_____

_____

_____

_____

_____

Now ask yourself, "How did I get through this without knowing prior to the event that I could do it?" Write down your responses here:

_____

_____

_____

_____

In reply to this question, it is not unusual for people to say that they sought strength and guidance from some greater power during this particular time. Some say that they prayed to Jesus, God, or a higher power to see them through and give them the strength and courage to go on. Others report that they amazed themselves by the way they responded with such calm bravery in such perilous situations. But most people confide that at some point during the ordeal, an inner strength and unexplainable power took over—a courage and strength that allowed them to persevere in spite of their fear with the confidence that there was something greater than their own pain and fear that was guiding them one step at a time. This is the moment in time when we accept universal guidance and protection, even though we may not quite understand it. It's when we stop the need to know.

Allow Yourself Not to Know

Stopping the _need_ to know is essential if you are to discover your True North and utilize your inner voice of wisdom and courage. I'm not saying that you should forget everything you know and let your mind go blank. I'm saying that you should not let _not knowing_ something in advance stop you from living your fullest, most extraordinary life.

It's okay to allow yourself the freedom not to know things. For example, sometimes knowing too much actually hinders our ability to do our best work. If I'd known ahead of time that the likelihood of my first two books becoming best-sellers was actually quite small, I might not have worked so hard to sell them at conferences all over the world, on the Internet, and in media interviews. But I didn't know my chances, so I kept pushing and going the extra mile to promote my books at every opportunity. I went along, day after day, fully expecting that the sales of my books would soar. I'm glad now that I didn't know any differently, nor did I have the need to know. But I'll tell you what I did know: I knew that I had complete control and authority *not* to let myself down as an author and to do my best work, no matter what the statistics revealed or how successful most first-time authors have been. I've always believed that trusting yourself and believing in yourself in the face of the unknown is the greatest security you can possess.

Here are some words of wisdom that I keep visible in my office and read each morning before I start my day.

Embracing Uncertainty Is . . .
Knowing before it is done,
Believing before it is proven,
Loving before you are loved,
Giving before you have received,
Embracing uncertainty is
Abandoning the need to know and
Trusting in the Universal Power of Faith.

—Author unknown

When you give up your need for certainty, you gain so much more—spontaneity, creativity, an adventuresome spirit, and an expanded awareness.

What We Lose in Certainty, We Gain in Expanded Awareness

Writer Anais Nin said that life shrinks or expands in proportion to one's courage. Do you choose to live an expansive life? Do you choose self-expression and adventure over fear or an abundance of caution?

Life expands or contracts to meet the expectations we place on it. When you start paying close attention to your inner voice of courage and valor, you expand your lens of perception, along with the realm of possibility. Here are three of my personal favorite "life expanders" to help you get started.

1. Travel
2. Read
3. Leap

Travel

Did you know that fewer than 4 percent of Americans hold passports and a much smaller fraction ever use them? Here's my advice: If you don't have a passport, get one. Suppose you had the opportunity to travel to Rome or Greece or Paris, but you had to be ready to leave tomorrow morning? If you didn't have a passport, you would miss out on seeing some of the world's most amazing sites, like the Roman Coliseum, the Parthenon, or the Eiffel Tower. When you miss the opportunity to travel, you contract your life awareness.

There is no greater life expander than travel. Travel makes us wake up to our life and say, "Guess what? The way we do things in my small corner of the world is not the way the rest of the world lives." Travel makes us more sensitive to others—their life struggles and hardships, their accomplishments, their political views, and their cultural values. If all you ever see of how other people live and behave is what's shown on the 6 o'clock news, you will never have an accurate picture of the collective soul of humanity and how that collective soul affects us all. If you see pictures of people in other lands on the news or in magazines, but you never sit and talk to some of those people face to face, how will you know what they are really feeling or thinking and what might connect your lives in ways you never imagined?

When we travel, we experience exhilaration and excitement. We develop our curiosity and higher levels of awareness. By exploring the planet we inhabit, we step into other people's maps of the world, and we begin to experience life from their perspective, not just our own. And that map of the world doesn't have to be thousands of miles away. On the contrary, it might be 15 miles away in a community you've never visited. It's not about the mileage you cover; it's about how far your heart and mind reach out to experience someone else's culture and appreciate how it differs from yours.

Although cultures may vary widely, our humanity is very much the same. It doesn't matter whether I am having lunch with a Kuwaiti woman, coffee with a man from Nigeria, dinner with a couple from the Netherlands, or a meeting with political figures from Washington, D.C. I've come to realize that we as humans all have the same basic desires—to see our children grow to be healthy and happy, to live our lives in peace, and to have our families and friends around us. These are the common denominators I have experienced among the lifelong friendships I have built through the years with people from all walks of life and religions. And it is in these commonalities that I have found hope for a better tomorrow.

My travels have given me the lifelong education of walking in other people's shoes and appreciating the hardships, losses, and longings of those who live outside my small community. I've seen firsthand how travel makes us better people—more compassionate and understanding. Travel gives us a new lens of perspective on what is most important to us and how we can make a difference in the world.

"My favorite thing is to go where I've never been."
—DIANE ARBUS, PHOTOGRAPHER

Travel also makes the world a much smaller place. We really do live in a global village. With the Internet and high-speed transportation, we can travel the globe in record-breaking time and take back with us a bounty of experience and knowledge that expands our horizons, ultimately making the world a better place.

So where have you ventured to lately outside of your own comfort zone? Where would you go if you could? Today? Right now?

If you have the resources, here's what I recommend: Get out of your environment and visit a place you have never been before—preferably one that's outside your own city, state, or even country. Maybe it's a place that will provide you with greater detail about your ethnicity and cultural heritage, or perhaps it will be a place that you have read about all of your life and dreamed of exploring. It doesn't matter. Just go somewhere other than your own surroundings.

If you're not so bold or you're not inclined to travel the world, then just make the decision to visit a nearby place that you've never been to. Maybe you can start with a day trip to a museum in a different city. Going a long distance isn't the goal. The goal is to broaden your awareness of new and different places, and to be open to other people and how their experiences differ from your own. You don't have to trek the Himalayas, although that would be a magnificent adventure; you can trek the historical walks in Boston or the bike trails of the American River in Sacramento, or you can walk or bike across the Golden Gate Bridge in San Francisco or explore the swamps of Louisiana. The goal is to expand your horizons, try new and exciting things, and eliminate the rigidity that so often seeps into our lives.

Life Expanders

- Get a passport, or renew the one you've got.
- Visit a foreign country.
- Visit a country where no one speaks your language.

> ➤ Plan a day trip to a place you've never been.
> ➤ Buy a globe. Close your eyes, spin the globe, and point to a world location, then go there.

Read

In the words of Dr. Seuss, "The more that you read, the more things you will know. The more that you learn, the more places you will go."

If you want to expand your life, then read as much and as often as you can and watch your life be transformed. For example, when you are faced with difficult times and tough decisions in your life—whether it's a divorce, developing political views, or working on personal growth issues—reading is one way of helping you to understand yourself better. In fact, you're doing that right now by reading this book. Whatever you may be facing, reading can show you alternative ways to handle life and become a more informed person.

"One sure window into a person's soul is his reading list."—MARY B. W. TABOR, JOURNALIST

If you believe in the power of timing, there are certain books and reading materials that seem to come into your life at just at the right moment. How many times, when you are reading something, have you thought to yourself, "This is the perfect time for me to be reading this"? Maybe a friend sent you a newspaper article in the mail, or you stumbled across a book on your bookshelf that you had completely forgotten you had, or you discovered a story on the Internet that changed your perception or your approach to something.

When I was a kid, I loved reading. There was a bookmobile that came by our neighborhood every Friday afternoon. If you had a library card, you could check out books, just like at the library, and then return them the following Friday. I loved that bookmobile. When other kids were looking for the ice cream truck, I was looking for the bookmobile.

"We read frequently, if unknowingly, in quest of a mind more original than our own."—HAROLD BLOOM, LITERARY CRITIC

One day while I was shopping with my parents, I asked my father if I could buy a book at the bookstore. I wanted to buy *The Diary of Anne Frank.* "Why buy the book, when you can get it at the library for free and read it?" was my father's response. I suppose, at the time, it never dawned on him that I might have wanted to keep that book and read it again someday, or just hold it and look at it for inspiration when the mood struck. The next day my mother went to the bookstore and bought me the book. On a recent business trip to Amsterdam, I visited the Anne Frank house and was inspired to do so because of that book. Decades later, *The Diary of Anne Frank* continues to expand and heighten my life awareness.

Rudy Giuliani, the former mayor of New York City, talks about the power of reading in his book *Leadership*, and how one of the ways he was able to lead in the face of the tragedy on September 11 was by reading Roy Jenkins's biography of Winston Churchill. Reading the biographies and autobiographies of people whom you admire and aspire to learn from can be life-altering. But sometimes we read just to expand our everyday interests and hobbies. Thus, when Rudy Giuliani decided to take up golf, he started out reading *Golf for Dummies,* by Gary McCord, moved on to David Pelz's *Short Game Bible*, and then went on to Ben Hogan's *Five Lessons: The Modern Fundamentals of Golf.*

Maybe you've done the same thing in expanding your life and self-directed learning. Perhaps you've read books on cooking in order to become a better cook, or books and magazines on aviation in order to become a better pilot.

And if you're unable to travel as you might like, then you can read about the places you've never been and, through the printed word, let the images take you there. As a young girl, I was always intrigued by the images created from the books I read—images of diverse and interesting cultures, like tribal women walking around with baskets on their heads, Egyptian priests tracing energy meridians in people with their wands, cowboys driving cattle in Texas, and Polynesian dancers telling stories with their hands. It was through reading that I first traveled the world, long before I ever bought an airplane ticket.

Today my house is filled with thousands of books, from the floor to the ceiling. I love the look, the feel, and the smell of old books and new books. From early childhood to today, reading has continued to expand my life awareness in quantum proportion.

Life Expanders

- ➤ Read a biography or a memoir of someone in history that you strongly admire.

- ➤ Subscribe to a publication you've never read before.

- ➤ Go to the bookstore and buy a book, any book.

- ➤ Read a newspaper not from your area.

- ➤ Visit an antiquarian bookstore; touch and smell the books.

- ➤ Read a great novel and then give it to someone else to read.

- ➤ Start or join a book club.

Leap

Maybe good things come to those who wait, but I believe that the best things come to those who seize the moment and make it their own by taking leaps of faith throughout their lives.

"Jump."—JOSEPH CAMPBELL, MYTHOLOGIST AND STORYTELLER

Never be afraid to be called a dreamer or an adventurer. Indulge yourself in your dreams and in taking leaps of faith. Push the outside of the envelope, test your senses, and don't be afraid to jump. So what if you went to college and got a degree in accounting—if you now want to become an opera singer, go for it. It's your life. I believe that when we live each day open to guidance from our True North, our greater purpose is revealed to us. And, yes, sometimes it can be frightening.

For instance, sure there are some people who have taken leaps of faith, only to face disaster or great disappointment. Three people who come to mind right off the

"I cannot live without books." —THOMAS JEFFERSON

top are Amelia Earhart, Dr. Martin Luther King, Jr., and Christa McAuliffe. While inspirational for their willingness to dream and take courageous risks, each lost her or his life in the pursuit of those dreams. But for every Earhart, King, or McAuliffe, there are thousands more who take leaps of faith and, by doing so, succeed in their quest to live their best lives and expand their realm of possibility.

Your particular leap of faith doesn't have to be extraordinary. It's not required that you find a cure for a dreaded disease or that you change the world for the better. Your leap, however, does have to change *your* world for the better.

Here's the litmus test for all leaps of faith: Does your leap of faith put to the test your physical, emotional, psychological, spiritual, or intellectual survival skills? If the answer to one or more of these is yes, then you are about to embark on a true leap of faith. But if you're looking for a safe and secure landing strip for the jump you're about to take, you may be wasting your time. Safety and security are super-

"The question should be, is it worth trying to do, not can it be done."—ALLARD LOWENSTEIN, POLITICAL ACTIVIST

stitions—nothing more, nothing less. If you're waiting for the safest and securest moment to come about before you take action, I'm here to tell you that that moment may never come.

All you have is right here and right now. That's it. By taking leaps of faith, we tell the world that we are embracing this moment in time and living our best life, right here and right now, without the promise or expectations of more, because all that we are in this moment in time is good enough, extraordinary, and miraculous.

As Albert Einstein said, "There are only two ways to live your life. One is as though nothing is a miracle. The other is as though everything is a miracle."

Taking leaps of faith isn't something that's reserved for the big risk takers or the wildly creative, so don't narrow your definition. You have the capacity to do this at whatever level is appropriate for you. All you have to do is to joyfully expand that capacity to include greater self-expression, desire, drive, and the grand exploration of greater possibilities. All that is required is that while you are on your journey to True North, you keep an open mind and an open heart.

> **"Those who lose dreaming are lost."—ABORIGINAL PROVERB**

Life Expanders

- ➤ Do something outside of your comfort zone.

- ➤ Fill in the blank: "I would shock everyone who knows me if I did this: _____."

> **"Shun the incremental and go for the leap." —JACK WELCH**

- ➤ Complete this sentence: "I've always wanted to

_____."

- ➤ Whatever your response to the previous bullet point was, go and do it!

- ➤ Repeat this affirmation to yourself: The best parachute packers are the ones who jump out of airplanes!

I hope that the navigation tools in Week 2 of this program have given you the inner direction and guidance necessary for honoring, respecting, and igniting your inner voice of wisdom and courage, and that by doing so, you will be better equipped to move forward in cultivating your life's greatest interests and desires, accepting fully that your journey toward True North is guaranteed to bring you unexpected surprises, enlightenment, and inner strength beyond your wildest imagination.

> **"Don't let them tame you!" —ISADORA DUNCAN**

5

Cultivating Interests Before Callings

Higher Purpose Statement

When you are pinpointing what it is you are most interested in becoming and what you'd like to spend your life doing, be honest with yourself. Acknowledge realistically where you are on the learning curve relative to where you want to be. Accept your shortcomings and weaknesses. Discover your gifts by excavating your strongest, most genuine interests and talents, without regard to what your parents, your friends, or other outside influences think you'd be good at. Explore your interests thoroughly, and imagine what it would be like to live those interests every day. Before you can experience a higher calling, there is an inside-out process that must take place. Start the process by identifying your strongest interests and framing them as your emotional and intellectual competencies. Allow these competencies to lead you toward your greatest passion and let your passion guide you toward your dreams. Then ask yourself this question: "Is this at all realistic?" If the answer is yes, you have found your authentic calling.

If You Are Being Called, Then Who's Doing the Calling?

In recent years, you may have read or heard a great deal about callings—heeding your life's calling, realizing your calling, being true to your calling. So here's my question: If you believe you are being called to do something with your life, who's doing the calling?

How many times have you read or heard about someone who believes that now is the time for him or her to start making major life changes, maybe letting go of a secure job or considering moving far away, because this person feels that he or she ought to be doing something else with his or her life? Are these really callings, or are these behaviors driven by the "ought tos" in our life, some kind of abstract code for trying to find True North?

Perhaps the most important vocational questions we can ask ourselves do not take the form of, "What ought I to do with my life?" Rather, they ask, "Who am I really?" "What does my life have in store for me based on my deepest interests?" "What am I truly capable of becoming based on my competencies? "What is my nature?"

Nurturing Your Nature

Everything in our universe has a nature. This implies that there are limits to everything and everyone, as well as great potential and capabilities that have yet to be discovered. If you are seeking a calling without first accepting and understanding the raw materials that you have to work with, what you create in your life may well turn out to be fake, awkward, and clumsy. To put it simply, none of us can perform at our highest level of potential when we are behaving and acting in contradiction to how we see ourselves or what we hold true.

Parents, friends, and even acquaintances may regularly tell you that you are smarter than Stephen Hawking or Bill Gates, better looking than Tom Cruise or Catherine Zeta-Jones, and wittier than Jerry Seinfeld. Those people may be telling you that you can do anything you want—anything you put your mind to. But here's the reality: You can't be anything you might want, but you *can* be anything you are truly capable of becoming. There's a huge difference between the two. One belief is based on fantasy and the other on reality. One belief sets you up for disappointment, and the other prepares you for success—success meaning greater internal happiness and contentment with your life and the way you spend your time.

Getting Real about Being Real

This chapter will help you to get real about what you are actually capable of becoming and will move you from simply seeking your calling to first understanding the emotional and intellectual competencies that lie within you—their limitations as well as their great capabilities. When we are honest about what we can become by maximizing the actual competencies we have within us, we are better equipped to find our True North. I believe that all of us have what I call a competency compass inside us—a powerful tool of your inner guidance system.

Great Expectations, or the Spirit of Self

When we are growing up, we are often surrounded by expectations of us—expectations that may have little to do with who we really are. These expectations may well be held by the people closest to us, such as friends and family, all of whom may have good intentions, but nevertheless may be trying to fit us into the mold that they think suits us best.

Over the years, everything that we experience in our families, our schools, our work environments, and our religious communities, including the desire to conform to images of acceptability can influence us greatly. This sometimes drives us even further away from who we really are in order to gain the approval of others. Here's an example I experienced firsthand of someone who was living in a culture that was filled with good intentions, but did not discern the spirit of self.

Being raised in a traditional Italian/Irish Catholic culture, we were often told stories about nuns and priests who were "called" to enter their sacred vocation. The interpretation of calling at that time implied that some divine messenger reached down to, let's say, an unsuspecting young girl who really wanted to be a Broadway actress—a girl who took years of dance lessons and spent all her money on acting workshops in order to pursue her passion, only to be plucked from the chorus line at her first audition, summoned by the heavens without warning, and told, "Sorry to interrupt, but in case you hadn't noticed, you're being 'called' to live a life of celibacy and join the convent." All right. Stop right here. Where's the passion? Where's the desire to pursue one's greatest interests and talents? How is this nurturing our nature? Is this an authentic calling, or is something else going on?

An Authentic Calling Starts with an Expression of Your Deepest Interests and Passion, Not Someone Else's

The story of the aspiring Broadway actress I'm referring to is true. When we were just 19 years old, my girlfriend Josie confided to me that she was certain that she'd received a "call," and that she was now going to relinquish all her hopes and dreams of singing and dancing on Broadway. She felt compelled to tell her parents and her priest what she'd experienced, and to turn in her tap shoes for short hair and a black habit.

Even back then, I knew that this was nuts. I'd known this girl all my life, and I was certain that joining the convent was not a genuine interest or inner desire of hers by a long shot. For her, as for most of us at that time, going to church wasn't a passion, it was a guilt trip. It wasn't about spirituality back then; it was about religion, rules, and the consequences of facing an angry God if you didn't do what was expected of you.

So my first question to Josie was this: "If you're hearing a calling, then who is doing the calling?" Of course, I got the answer I was expecting. My friend's assumption was that it was God that was doing the calling. I didn't buy this explanation then, and I still don't.

I just couldn't believe that God, or any higher power, would bless someone with so much natural talent, a burning desire to use that talent, and a genuine, deep-down interest in using it, only to squelch that talent in that person's youth, pulling her in a direction that she'd never considered, or had any inclination to pursue in the first place.

Do I believe that my friend really did experience a calling? Yes. But the calling wasn't coming from spirit, it was coming from her parents and their desire to have someone in the family pursue a life of holiness and religious vocation. In those days, especially in certain religious cultures, having a child who chose a path of church service and a life of piety was seen as practically guaranteeing the entire family entry into heaven. It was also considered very prestigious in certain ethnic communities to have a son or daughter join the elite ranks of priesthood or nun-hood. By association, this somehow made everyone closer to God, except perhaps the person her- or himself if, like Josie, she or he was about to embark on a less than authentic calling.

Please don't misunderstand me. I absolutely believe in callings—authentic callings that speak to people in many ways, whether what the person is being called to is a life of ministering to others through the church or other nonprofit services or of practicing medicine in a remote jungle of a third-world country. The point I am making is that it is critical that each of us conduct a closer examination of just what we think our true calling is and initiate an inside-out process that can help us determine whether that calling is truly one of deep-down personal interest or whether it is influenced by the expectations of others.

I'm convinced to this day that my friend's calling was really a subtle but strong message that she had received from her family throughout her lifetime, gently urging her to become what they hoped she would become. It soon became evident that the desire to be the good daughter who made the ideal vocational decision won out, even if it meant betraying the person that Josie was born to be.

The next 6 years of Josie's life were spent following a calling that was never hers to begin with, while her true calling, to be a Broadway star, was no longer considered. All those dreams and passion lay dormant, but they were not dead.

Eventually, Josie's real interests and talents were reignited when she became the drama and theater coach at an all-girls Catholic high school. But that wasn't enough to satisfy her natural desire to live her dreams and pursue her strongest interest. As a result, Josie became increasingly unhappy, depressed, and frustrated with her life. Why? She wasn't nurturing her nature as God had really intended. Instead, she was acting in a manner that was inconsistent with who she really was and who had prepared herself to become. And whenever we live in a way that just doesn't feel right, we begin concealing and ignoring parts of ourselves that long to be acknowledged, which only creates a greater emptiness within as we push our innermost desires to the rear of our awareness.

Denying our inner truth and our authentic selves is like trying to keep the lid on a pressure cooker that has built up too much steam. You can try as much as you like, but containing all that built-up steam will be next to impossible. After spending almost a decade as a nun, Josie left the convent, moved to New York, and 6 months later auditioned for an off-Broadway musical. She got the part, and she continues to live and work in the city's theater community to this day. When Josie began nurturing her nature by once again paying attention to her deepest interests and dusting off her inherent talents, she was able to take the first step in a process that would ultimately lead to her authentic purpose and highest calling. She found the courage to start living from the inside out, and she hasn't stopped since.

Activating Your Inner Guidance System

The word *vocation* is rooted in a Latin word meaning "voice"—and this is not the voice of what others expect of you, or the standards by which others may believe you should be living your life. It is the voice that speaks from within you and you alone—a voice that speaks to your higher truth and identity. This implies that our vocation is not a goal or career objective to pursue and achieve in this lifetime. Rather, it is a birthright—a gift to be received and accepted with great appreciation. In this chapter you will find that this gift goes hand in hand with the quest to discover your True North, and that you begin by activating four Life Compasses in your inner guidance system that can help guide you to the life you were meant to live and the vocation you were meant to follow. These four Life Compasses are (1) identifying interests and framing them as competencies, (2) allowing your competencies to lead you toward your passion, (3) letting your passion guide you to your dreams, and (4) navigating toward your true calling. With each Life Compass you will find worksheets and exercises for conducting your own inside-out process.

Connecting Who You Are with What You'd Like to Do

Your higher calling is your greater purpose, only more vocationally focused. When you experience a powerful sense of passion and interest in your work, you are more likely to love what you do and excel at it. The path this takes looks different for each of us.

Not everyone has the desire or calling to save the world, win a Pulitzer prize, climb Mount Everest, or achieve fame and fortune as a movie star. You and you alone must determine what the right path for you will be. Maybe that means taking a job as an elevator mechanic, working as an organic farmer, driving a taxi, or painting houses for a living.

My friend Nancy reminded me of a poignant scene from the 1954 movie classic *Sabrina,* starring Audrey Hepburn and Humphrey Bogart. In this scene, Sabrina expresses her admiration for her father, the longtime devoted chauffeur for the wealthy Larrabee family, by telling him, "Do you know what I love best about you? That you decided to become a chauffeur because you wanted to have time to read." It is in this moment that Sabrina's father's calling is revealed. The man loved to read—that was his passion, his interest, his greatest desire. What other job would have afforded him the opportunity to read endlessly while waiting in a long succession of cars for his employer to return from lengthy meeting after lengthy meeting?

There are thousands of callings, and we have just as many reasons for expressing them and the more significant purpose and quest for our individual happiness. The point is this: You should never limit yourself by doing what you think you *should* do. Instead, you should fully explore your interests and abilities, then align these with your passions, which will in turn lead you to your higher purpose, or calling.

The more honest you are with yourself and others about who you are and what you are capable of becoming, the more likely you will be to live your best life. Why? Because when we purposely align our outer behavior with our inner truth, life flows in a direction that is more meaningful and rewarding. In addition, we stop wasting time and energy on denial, suppression, and anger, and instead we gain insight, clarity of purpose, and an evolution of our soul.

Let's start with your first Life Compass to help you bring your inner and outer worlds closer together. After completing this section, you will find that when the two worlds are congruent, the pieces of your life just seem to fit better.

LIFE COMPASS: *Pinpointing Your Emotional and Intellectual Competencies*

How do you go about choosing a life that expresses all that you can be? The first step is to identify and detail your human competencies.

Webster's dictionary defines *competency* or *competence* as "having the possession of a required skill, qualification, or capacity; having suitable or sufficient skill, knowledge, experience, etc. for some purpose." But competency actually has many more meanings when it comes to pinpointing our attributes, or to describing the characteristics of people, such as values, humor, listening skills, compassion, adaptability, self-confidence, and influence. In my seminars, I refer to this as a person's Attribute Bundle—a collection of all these competencies put together.

Why is it important for us to pinpoint our competencies and attributes? When we take time to do this, we begin a process that brings us closer to living the life we were meant to live because our outer behavior is fueled by our inner truth and authenticity. We see ourselves leading a life of dignity and self-respect, and there is no pretense to maintain because everything we do reflects our beliefs and what we know to be true.

Competencies can easily be divided into two areas: (1) your emotional, human capabilities, or soft-skill competencies, and (2) your intellectual, practical, or hard-skill competencies. The key is to identify both skill sets and then align them to the vocational calling you desire.

Why am I asking you to list two sets of competencies, one emotional and one intellectual? Because neither set can be completely separated from the other. Perhaps you are heavily into technical work. Let's say your background is in engineering and your education and work skills are highly technical and scientific. If your ultimate interest is to one day head up a scientific study at MIT and lead a group of researchers in designing a specific project, your technical know-how, education, training, and analytical thinking would represent one set of competencies that would align you to this type of work. But they will not be enough to ensure your long-term success if, on the emotional, soft-skill side of the equation, you are lacking in the ability to influence others, collaborate with team members, listen and give accurate feedback with patience and consideration, and meet deadlines. If you ignore these other critical competencies, you will fall far short of performing at the level required to do the job successfully and achieve optimum satisfaction. Both your emotional and intellectual competencies should dovetail and be in alignment with your dream in order for you to achieve your higher calling.

Next, you will find a sample worksheet for identifying both your emotional, soft-skill competencies and your intellectual, hard-skill competencies, and a model for framing them for greater clarity. The sample given represents the responses from one of my seminar participants, a woman of about 34 years of age who very much wanted to make a life change in her career. Review her approach to using this Life Compass and then go on to complete your own worksheet and exercises.

Sample Worksheet
Contributed in a workshop by Marianne T., Sioux City, Iowa

Identifying Your Emotional/Soft-Skill Competencies and Your Intellectual/Hard-Skill Competencies

My Strongest Interests, Talents, and Human Characteristics (Soft Skills)	My Technical Skills, Cognitive Ability, Education, and Experience Skill Sets (Hard Skills)
Caring for others	Asst. project manager—
Growing things	2 years experience
Influencing young minds	BS degree in engineering
Being humorous	Critical thinker
Entertaining	Good implementing strategy
Listening	Keen understanding of sciences
Coaching teams	and mathematics
Finding solutions	Precise in my work
Mediating	Technical writing
Heading up and completing projects	Projecting and meeting deadlines
Envisioning possibilities	

If I Had a Dream Job, It Would Be

To become a middle-school guidance counselor for emotionally challenged students, ages 12 to 14, to create a school program dedicated to building self-esteem among students of all backgrounds, and to follow up and measure these students' ongoing success and progress over a period of 10 years. I would then like to use this study as a basis for pursuing my doctorate in counseling.

My Present Job Is

Working as an assistant project manager in a high-tech company that manufactures software programs worldwide.

Realistically, Am I Equipped to Do the Work I Am Being Called to Do? Do I Possess the Basic Competencies That Will Allow Me to Develop Myself to This Higher Calling?

At present I do not possess the qualifications necessary for this work. However, I do possess the basic competencies that will allow me to be successful in this field, provided that I am willing to make a commitment to obtaining the appropriate educational training and skills development that will get me there. I am confident that I can do this.

Where Am I on the Learning Curve in Order to Get There? How Much Time Will I Require to Get Myself Up to Speed?

I would first need to return to school and get my master's degree and teaching credential in counseling. I would do this in the evenings, and I estimate that it will take me approximately 3 years to complete this if I pursue my degree online or through a distance learning program. I have identified four potential universities and financial aid programs that meet my needs. In the meantime, I will volunteer one weekend a month at my local middle school, helping to create a self-esteem program for students and developing a measurement system that the school will be able to use for ongoing improvement and learning purposes.

Worksheet

After reviewing the previous sample worksheet, take time to complete the following framework for yourself.

Identifying Your Emotional/Soft-Skill Competencies and Your Intellectual/Hard-Skill Competencies

My Strongest Interests, Talents, and Human Characteristics (Soft Skills)	My Technical Skills, Cognitive Ability, Education, and Experience Skill Sets (Hard Skills)
_____	_____
_____	_____
_____	_____
_____	_____
_____	_____
_____	_____
_____	_____
_____	_____
_____	_____
_____	_____

Note: If you get stuck, it is all right to ask others to describe what they perceive to be some of your strongest talents and skills. But remember, ultimately, it is what you feel inside that will count most.

If I Had a Dream Job, It Would Be

_____

_____

_____

_____

_____

My Present Job Is

_____

_____

Realistically, Am I Equipped to Do the Work I Am Being Called to Do? Do I Possess the Basic Competencies That Will Allow Me to Develop Myself to This Higher Calling?

_____

_____

_____

_____

_____

Where Am I on the Learning Curve in Order to Get There? How Much Time Will It Require to Get Myself Up to Speed?

_____   _____

_____   _____

_____   _____

_____   _____

_____   _____

NAVIGATION TOOL: _The Powerful Use of Competencies in the Real World_

In our global economy and workplace, the word _competency_ can have many interpretations. These meanings can sometimes be related to tasks and results, such as making deals, organizing things, crunching the numbers, or retooling work environments. Other times they can describe characteristics or behaviors of the people doing the job, such as a person's awakening spirit, outgoing nature, outrageous sense of humor, artistic talents, or ability to influence and affect change.

When we take the time to identify our vast array of competencies and talents, we uncover a powerful vocational tool that can provide the key that will unlock greater opportunities and vocational choices that we might make along the way. Listed here are a few ways in which your own competencies can be used as helpful vocational decision-making tools:

Review your competencies and interests from the previous exercise and let them guide you when you are faced with vocational choices, such as:

1. Rewriting your job description or detailing your vision of a new career opportunity

2. Creating and launching new projects

3. Deciding whether or not to start your own business

4. Choosing a graduate school program that fits your best interests and needs

5. Selecting appropriate training seminars to attend

6. Choosing team members for a project you are heading up

7. Developing a strategic career plan

8. Deciding to write a book or become a subject matter expert

Add more of your own ideas to the list here:

9. _____

10. _____

11. _____

12. _____

NAVIGATIONAL TOOL: *10 Premium Emotional and Soft-Skill Competencies*

Technical, intellectual, and hard-skill competencies are typically the easiest for us to clarify. Why? Because we already know what our experiences have been up to this point, where we've worked, and what we've accomplished. Most of us can quickly state our level of education, our work skills, and the tasks required of us if we are to perform well on the job. However, studies have shown time and again that even for the most technical gurus, the most important competencies that they can possess, competencies that will help ensure their success, will be in the category of human capability, emotional, or soft-skills intelligence. But identifying these capabilities can sometimes give us the most difficulty.

For this reason, listed for you here are 10 examples of premium emotional and soft-skill competencies. These premium competencies have been most frequently selected over time by hundreds of my workshop and seminar participants when they were asked to choose the core soft-skill competencies that are most critical to a person's long-term success and happiness. The exercises that follow are based on a wide variety of participants' input, questions, and intended application of these competencies.

Let this sample list serve as a navigation tool in achieving higher awareness of the critical soft-skill competencies in your own Attribute Bundle.

You'll also find that the list offers a starting point from which you can begin to build your own customized premium competencies and create a framework from which you can adapt and define a model for applying them to your specific vocational needs. This list was developed to get you started.

1. Integrity

2. Trust and values

3. Relationship building

4. Listening

5. Influencing

6. Spirit

7. Passion and intuition

8. Setting priorities

9. Sense of humor

10. Vision and adaptability

Why am I calling this a list of soft-skill competencies and not core values? Because when the competencies in this list are acted upon, they represent more than our principles and values; they represent what we care most about and how we live our lives.

NAVIGATION TOOL: *Making Premium Soft-Skill Competencies Work for You*

Our behaviors and our individual characteristics are competency indicators. Your outer behavior is fueled by your inner truth. What you do and the actions you take reflect what you believe in, how you feel about things, and what you know to be true up to this moment in time.

Describing Behaviors and Characteristics

For each of the emotional and soft-skill competencies in the list, provide a brief description of how you would demonstrate and apply this behavior in your dream job, and what each behavior represents as a vocational characteristic from your personal perspective. If you need help, move forward to the exercise "A Model for Expanding Premium Competencies" for more ideas.

INTEGRITY

_____

_____

TRUST AND VALUES

_____

_____

RELATIONSHIP BUILDING

_____

_____

LISTENING

_____

_____

INFLUENCING

_____

_____

SPIRIT (competitive spirit, energy, positive influence, higher consciousness)

_____

_____

PASSION AND INTUITION

_____

_____

SETTING PRIORITIES AND MAKING IMPORTANT DECISIONS

_____

_____

SENSE OF HUMOR

_____

_____

VISION AND ADAPTABILITY

_____

_____

Complete this exercise by adding your own premium soft-skill competencies to the list and providing a brief description of how you would demonstrate and apply each behavior to your dream job, and what each behavior represents as a vocational characteristic from your personal perspective.

NAVIGATION TOOL: _A Model for Expanding Premium Competencies_

Premium competencies connect our career-planning strategies with our core values and behaviors.

Answer these questions and perform the exercises on the top 10 premium soft-skill competencies. Watch this become a powerful navigation tool that you can use to link your premium soft-skill competencies to your intellectual and hard-skill competencies when determining your greatest capabilities and gifts.

1. *Integrity*

Our integrity tells the world who we are and what we care most about. Integrity is not simply an expansion of human honesty and trustworthiness; it is what remains when we strip away all of our credentials and reputation. It's our moral consciousness, our principal beliefs and values. And as Elizabeth Dole, former president and CEO of the American Red Cross, once said, "Integrity is the one thing every person has 100 percent control over."

Exercise

If integrity were a crime and you were arrested for having it, would there be enough evidence to convict you? Write down the undeniable evidence against you. State how you live and lead with integrity. Be as specific as possible in your response.

_____

_____

_____

_____

_____

Behavioral characteristics of integrity include open and honest communication, providing helpful feedback to others, recognizing and rewarding others, behaving ethically, walking the talk, and doing what you say you're going to do.

2. *Trust and Values*

When we break our promises, we erode trust and we lose credibility—both of which are incredibly difficult to regain once they are lost. The cornerstones of trust include the following:

➤ Doing what you say you're going to do

➤ Respecting others and appreciating their differences

➤ Communicating openly

➤ Acknowledging that trust is a mutual exchange

Trust Exercise

Respond to the following questions regarding trust.

➤ Can you think of a time when trust was lost in your home or work environment?

_____

➤ What was the situation?

_____

➤ What were the consequences?

_____

➤ Was trust easily regained? If not, why not?

_____

➤ What do you think trust has to do with values and integrity?

_____

_____

_____

_____

_____

It is said that our values are the guardian angels of our integrity. Values are important because they define our desired behaviors through our personal conduct. Our values are woven into the fabric of our authentic selves: who we are, what we stand for, and what we hope to become.

Values Exercise

From the following list, circle the three things that you value most.

Friendships	Family relationships	Accountability
Advancement	Authority	Loyalty
Passion	Personal growth	Status
Self-respect	Excellence	Truth
Community	Wealth	Professional growth
Competence	Compensation	Competition
Home	Ethics	Achievement
Quality	Integrity	Trust
Honor	Respect	Courage

After you have selected the three areas you value most, answer the following questions:

How do you demonstrate on a daily basis that these are the core values by which you live your life?

Do you need to improve how you demonstrate your values in any of these three areas? If yes, how will you do this?

_____ _____

_____ _____

_____ _____

Do you believe that values can be learned? If yes, how would you teach them to others? How would you measure your effectiveness?

_____

_____ _____

_____

_____ _____

_____ _____

_____ _____

It is critical that a person's core values be in alignment with the core values of his or her higher calling. After completing this exercise, you will be better able to examine any possible discrepancies that may exist between the two and then work toward closing any gaps that you may uncover.

3. Relationship Building

Healthy relationships are important to both our personal and our professional success. Relationship building requires taking on more responsibility and being accountable for our actions. Here are some reasons why relationship building is an important soft-skill competency:

1. Relationships give people a sense of belonging.

2. Being part of a supportive relationship can be energizing and motivating.

3. It is within our relationships that we are often able to solve our greatest problems and deal with our fears.

Exercise

Here are six questions to ask yourself about building relationships.

1. What can I be doing more of to keep my relationships healthy and happy?

   _____

   _____

2. Am I a consistent contributor to my relationships, or do I expect more than I give?

   _____

   _____

3. What do I do best in a relationship?

   _____

   _____

4. What can I do right now to be a better friend, coworker, sister, brother, wife, father, or employer?

   _____

   _____

5. On a scale of 1 to 10, how would I rate as a relationship builder among those who know me?

   _____

   _____

6. Why would anyone want to be in a relationship with me? What's in it for them?

   _____

   _____

Do you possess the necessary characteristics for building stronger relationships? Can you answer yes to the following statements?

1. I nourish and instill pride in others.

2. I am supportive, and I listen.

3. I am empathetic and compassionate.

4. I encourage and influence others to be their best.

5. I always seek, and often find, a win-win solution when there is conflict.

6. I respect and welcome others' opinions and differences

4. *Listening*

Listening is an art. Listening is a skill. Listening is a character-building strength. Listening can be a person's most effective and influential navigation tool. Good listeners don't just wait for their turn to talk next. They make others feel important, worthy, and respected. Good listeners are other-centered.

Exercise

The following is a list of some of the ways in which good listeners behave. To demonstrate the effectiveness of listening behaviors, create an additional list of some of the ways in which people choose not to listen. Write down the behaviors and actions that would demonstrate that a person is a poor listener. Knowing what *not* to do when listening to someone can be just as valuable as knowing how to listen well.

Actions of good listeners include:

➤ Making eye contact

➤ Assuming the listening position—sitting up straight, leaning forward, taking notes

➤ Enjoying listening

➤ Giving your undivided attention

➤ Asking questions

_____

_____

_____

➤ How do you practice listening well? How do you know when others believe you are listening to them?

_____

_____

_____

5. Influencing and Persuading

These are both powerful soft-skill competencies. Think of a time when you may have been influential in a situation that required your leadership. What persuasive techniques did you use in this situation?

Exercise

The following are influential and persuasive behaviors. Why do you think these particular behaviors are important to building soft-skill competencies?

➤ Using sound reasoning to persuade others

➤ Writing clearly and with a convincing tone

➤ Using body language and voice inflection to influence others

➤ Consistently gaining supportive views and opinions

➤ Effectively overcoming objections and concerns

➤ Using tact at all times

➤ Demonstrating persuasive and articulate presentation skills

➤ Knowing the facts

➤ Never gossiping

---

6. Spirit (Competitive Spirit, Energy, Positive Influence, Higher Consciousness)

This competency describes the kind of person who is driven to be the best at whatever he or she does, whether that be through the spirit of robust competition or through injecting into others a contagious enthusiasm to accomplish the most difficult of tasks. People with spirit possess high energy and enthusiasm, whether it's for their job, a hobby, their spiritual life, or a sporting event. Spirit is a contagious emotional competency!

Exercise

Acknowledge your spirit.

Spirit means life. Bringing together our life and our livelihood is what brings our spirit alive. Having spirit requires having purpose, feeling joy, contributing at a greater, higher level than ever before, and living in depth, not just on the surface.

How would you describe your spirit? Describe a time when you put both your heart and your mind completely into an endeavor that resulted in spiritual fulfillment or a higher level of energy and consciousness. What impact did you have on those around you? What were the results?

---

7. *Passion and Intuition*

Our passions are the issues we care most deeply about—the issues we lie awake at night obsessing over. When we connect our interests and gifts with our passions, we gain a clearer perspective on what we are here to do and why. We have a defined reason for getting up each morning.

Passionate individuals not only lead but inspire. They strive against all odds to make their dreams and hopes reality. Passion is an emotional competency that was once possessed by Walt Disney and John F. Kennedy, Jr. It's a competency possessed today by leaders such as General Colin Powell, whose passion is the future of children in this nation, and Amazon.com's Jeff Bezos, whose passion continues to be changing the economics of the book industry by building the biggest bookstore in the world online.

Passion Exercise

Answer these questions about your passion.

1. What are you a passionate advocate for?

   _____

2. In what areas are you passionate about pursuing your talents and dreams?

   _____

3. Who are the passionate people with whom you surround yourself?

   _____

4. What issues or causes move you?

   _____

Intuition as an Emotional Competency

Albert Einstein once said, "The really valuable thing is intuition." But Einstein was decades ahead of his time. Only in recent years has intuition finally become a credible soft-skill competency, one that is actually being taught in leadership classes and graduate schools around the world. We've slowly learned that by trusting our gut feelings, we develop a keener perception and judgment about our work and our personal lives.

Intuition Exercise

When you have a hunch, do you follow up on it? Describe a time when you pursued a hunch. What was the outcome? Has there ever been a time when you regretted not relying more on your intuitive self? What happened?

_____

_____

_____

_____

_____

Characteristics of people who practice using their intuitive compass and gut instincts include taking risks, having faith in the unknown, believing in oneself, trusting instinctively, taking the leap of faith for an important cause, possessing a vision of what is yet to be, and relying on that small voice from within, or calling. Carefully consider this premium competency in both your personal and your professional life, and ask yourself if you are truly making the most of your intuitive talents.

8. *Setting Priorities*

Some people may think that setting priorities is more of an intellectual or hard skill because it requires keen decision-making abilities. I suppose it could be considered an intellectual competency, but I'd like you to consider it to be an emotional competency first, for several reasons. For one thing, establishing priorities often involves instinct and gut-level decision making, and can sometimes find us crossing some very emotional boundaries. Setting priorities can also be an art. Everyone has a different set of priorities. The question is, are your priorities in alignment with your becoming all that you can be and moving toward your higher self and your greater potential? When you live authentically, you know what you stand for, and, therefore, you make conscious choices. Your highest priorities will consistently get the lion's share of your time and attention. And that should mean that your behaviors are consistent with your beliefs. Are they?

Exercise

There are two ways to determine how you rank the importance of your priorities and the attention you give them. For a fast and accurate evaluation of what is most important to you in your life, take out your business calendar—i.e., your Palm Pilot, Daytimer, Day Runner, or whatever. Then get your personal checkbook or a recent check register. How you are spending your time and your money? That is the best indicator of how you are setting your priorities at this particular time in your life. For example, if you claim that your life's highest priority is your family, but your calendar shows that you're traveling 3 weeks of the month, 12 months of the year, perhaps your family isn't as great a priority as your work has become. And if you claim that one of your life priorities is saving to buy a new home, but your bank account clearly indicates that weekend getaways, designer clothes, and gourmet dining uses up most of this month's discretionary income, then perhaps the new home isn't as important to you as you say it is. How we spend our precious time and our money clearly demonstrates what we hold to be most important in our lives. What do you claim as your most important life priorities? Do your calendar and your bank account substantiate those claims?

_____

_____

_____

9. *Sense of Humor*

People with a sense of humor possess a human quality that is undeniably attractive and approachable to those around them. When a person uses humor in his or her life, he or she automatically relieves the pressures of the daily grind by releasing tension and instilling a feeling of camaraderie among those around him or her.

What kind of message is a CEO who dresses up like Elvis to give a speech or wears a Donald Duck or Mickey Mouse tie to a quarterly employees' luncheon sending out to his people? Perhaps he wants his employees to take themselves less seriously, smile more, laugh out loud, or just relax upon meeting him. It's okay to take your calling seriously and yourself lightly.

Use the following exercise to share examples of the humorous things you do to put people at ease and how you've gotten humor to work for you in a positive way.

Exercise

List three ways in which your humorous side helps to create a fun and positive environment for others—at home or at work. What are the benefits? Examples might include reducing stress, building camaraderie, lessening burnout, or eliminating tension.

    1. Example: _____

       Home/Workplace Benefits: _____

    2. Example: _____

       Home/Workplace Benefits: _____

    3. Example: _____

       Home/Workplace Benefits: _____

Humor may look different for each individual. Some folks tell jokes; others have a dry sense of humor that takes getting used to, but can be just as effective and lighthearted. Others use puns, and still others just poke fun at themselves. Acting just plain silly is yet another way to show your human side.

10. *Vision and Adaptability*

Vision and adaptability are premium competencies that go hand in hand. They help us to initiate and accept change. Without vision and the ability to adapt to it, a person's sense of purpose can be lost.

It is important that your vision and your attitude in adapting to that vision represent the collective aspirations, dreams, and desires of your higher purpose and calling. Inspiring a shared vision among those you love and those with whom you work can help sustain relationships through good times and bad.

All of the previous competencies will help provide you with the necessary foundation for actually creating and communicating your vision with greater clarity and passion.

Exercise

Try this vision exercise to adapt and build your talents when communicating a vision:

1. Is your vision eluding others because it is so far-reaching and nonspecific? What can you do to clearly define your vision so that others can visualize the big picture?

   _____

2. Ask others if they truly understand how your vision specifically relates to them. Be prepared to explain this.

   _____

3. What effective ways can you think of to better communicate your vision to those around you? What about using more descriptive language? Do you paint a vivid and exciting picture with the words you use? How do you engage your audience?

   _____

   _____

   _____

Visionary people see with their hearts and minds, as well as with their eyes. They articulate their vision so that everyone feels a part of it. And they can inspire others to buy into their vision because they are credible and trustworthy.

As a result of completing these exercises and ultimately better understanding the important role that premium competencies like these can play in your life, you will soon find yourself better able to:

➤ Build more cohesive and productive relationships, both personally and professionally

➤ Incorporate many of these soft-skill competencies into your quest to discover your True North

➤ Create and contribute to an environment in which trust and loyalty can be honored and renewed

➤ Instill confidence in those around you and encourage others to develop and practice their own list of premium soft-skill competencies

Getting It Together, Getting It in Alignment

Our core competencies help us to connect our vocational strategies to who we really are and what we believe we are called to do. When you are in alignment with your vocational aspirations, you will be better equipped to meet the challenges that are part of today's high-speed, global workplace head on, while continuing to move toward your dreams and a more purposeful life.

LIFE COMPASS: *Let Your Competencies Lead You toward Your Passion*

Here is where you will review the lists you've made of both your emotional, soft-skill competencies and your intellectual, hard-skill competencies. What do these lists tell you about yourself? What do the exercises you've completed reveal about you?

Knowing what you know now, how capable of pursuing your dream vocation do you feel? Is what you are capable of becoming in alignment with your competencies and desires? Once these areas are in alignment, you will begin to see that your competencies are an effective navigational tool for leading you toward your greatest passions. Why? Because it is human nature to want to throw ourselves into things where can we thrive, come alive, feel good about ourselves, exhibit exceptional talents and extraordinary interests, and feel exhilarated, not just once in a while, but most of the time.

Here's something else that it's important to know about passions: They're not passions if they don't move you! That's the ultimate test: Does whatever you think your passion is move you? Does the experience feel like an electrical undercurrent in your life whenever you're exposed to it? If the answer is yes, then you may well have found your passion.

Respond to the following:

This is my passion:

_____

This is why my passion moves me:

_____

_____

_____

What am I constantly drawn to, reading about, or talking to people about? Are these things connected to my passion?

_____

_____

_____

If I were to live my passion, this is what my life would look like:

_____

_____

_____

What is the greatest gratification and satisfaction that I would get from living my passion?

_____

_____

_____

All of the commonalities that emerge from your answers and from working your Life Compass exercises will give you a much clearer sense of what your passions really are.

Sample Worksheet
Contributed in a workshop by John M., Detroit, Michigan

LIFE COMPASS: *Steering Your Passion toward Your Dreams*

My Passions

Examples

I love reading. I spend hours in bookstores and several hundred dollars a month on new books for my library. Reading is one of my greatest passions.

I am crazy about books, old and new. I love how they look, how they smell, how they feel.

I was passionate about being the editor of my college newspaper for 2 years, and I worked day and night at that job because I loved it.

I'm excited beyond words about one day taking a sabbatical from my teaching job and writing a novel. I think about this all the time, and I have begun writing a proposal for a literary agent. I'm determined to make this happen within the next 5 years.

How My Passions Translate to My Higher Calling and My Dreams

Examples

For years I have dreamed of writing a best-selling novel. I think about it every single day, without exception. I know there is a bigger reason for my wanting to do this than just getting published. I have an inaudible voice within me that speaks to my filling a great literary gap in my lifetime.

I believe I have a calling to influence the publishing industry and to become involved in a series of projects and books that will influence people internationally.

I envision myself at book signings all around the country. I see myself speaking to large audiences of people and being interviewed on network talk shows, sharing my expertise.

Worksheet

In the sample worksheet, can you see how over the years John has continued to steer his passions toward his dreams? Do you see the consistency in motion between the two? Now it's your turn. How will you steer your passion toward your dreams?

LIFE COMPASS: *Steering Your Passion toward Your Dreams*

My Passions	*How My Passions Translate to My Higher Calling and My Dreams*
Example	**Example**
_____	_____
_____	_____
_____	_____
_____	_____
_____	**Example**
Example	_____
_____	_____
_____	_____
_____	_____
_____	_____

What If I'm Still Not in Alignment?

If you're still having a difficult time getting into alignment with your higher purpose, don't worry about it. It takes longer for some people than for others. There is no right or wrong way to go about this, and there is no right or wrong time frame in which you will discover the answers you are seeking.

Remember, most of us got sidetracked somewhere along the line. We silenced the voice within us that speaks to us about what we really want and what really matters. Perhaps along the way you've made choices, or had someone make them for you, that were driven by more practical matters. Maybe you set your dreams aside to make a living, or simply to survive. If this is the case, it may take you more time and focus to get clear about those original dreams and desires that are lying deep within you—perhaps dormant, but not dead.

The good news is that your inner wisdom never goes away, and it can be revived over time. Use this chapter to activate the innate knowing and inner urges that guided you when you were young. Then answer these questions.

If you feel that your competencies and your vocational calling are not in alignment, why do you think that is? What can you do to align these two areas as soon as possible? Have you considered meditating to get a clear flow of thoughts and ideas moving? What obstacles are getting in your way, or preventing you from excavating your inner desires? How can you work around these barriers? Go back and revisit the exercises in this chapter. Ask someone close to you, someone whom you trust and whose opinions you value, to assist you with this process. Sometimes it takes an objective party to see the match and uncover your hidden potential.

Write down the names of people who can help you in this process. They don't have to be in your city. This can be done by phone, fax, or email.

_____

_____

_____

_____

_____

Make notes here on any other ideas you have regarding ways to expedite the process.

_____

_____

_____

_____

_____

_____

_____

_____

_____

LIFE COMPASS: *Navigating toward Your True Calling*

You've taken the time to identify your strongest interests and then frame them as your emotional and intellectual competencies—the things you are truly capable of acting on. Next, you let your competencies move you toward your inner passion. Now it is time to see whether what you have excavated and examined holds up to the ultimate question: Is this at all realistic? Can you make it happen? If you make it happen, will you be living your dream and fulfilling your highest potential at this time in your life? If the answers to these questions are yes, you have met your calling and your calling has met you.

At this time and at this place in my life, I believe that this is my calling:

_____

_____

_____

_____

_____

Why I know that it is my calling that is speaking to me and not someone else:

_____

Ways in which I will honor my calling:

_____

How I will live a more authentic life as a result:

_____

Living an Authentic Life Takes Courage

When you discover your True North, you will be living your most authentic life. And that requires having the courage to face the truth about ourselves—who we really are and what we are truly capable of becoming.

Sometimes being truthful with ourselves is painful, because it can bring to the surface how we really feel about ourselves, or it can unlatch the fears that have been blocking our success, spotlight habits that are perpetuating the life we currently lead but want to change, or acknowledge the long-awaited dreams that we have suppressed. But, until we start taking action based on our inner truth and competencies, we will never experience real happiness or harmony. And doing this starts by living a life from the inside out.

Realization of the greater potential and happiness in your vocation and career will ultimately come when you begin to marry your deepest interests and competencies with the greater needs of the world around you. By doing this, we discover the joy of knowing that we are here to co-create a better world and that each of us does this in her or his own unique way and in her or his own time frame.

6

Pace Yourself—Life Isn't an All-or-Nothing Proposition

Higher Purpose Statement

Practice the art of good timing in your life. Trust the process, knowing that timing is everything. Respect the rhythm with which your life moves and unfolds. Be confident that you are in the perfect place at the perfect time, doing the best you can given your present capacity and level of awareness. Appreciate and work with the natural cycles and stages of life. Pace yourself—don't try to do everything all at once—but do something. Be kind, patient, and gentle with yourself. Move one step at a time into your own equilibrium and sense of momentum.

I Brake for Patience and Stillness

Some years ago in the United States, there was a memorable series of bumper stickers that carried a variety of messages, such as "I brake for kids" or "I brake for bicycles," and then there was the most popular of all these stickers, which read, "I brake for whales"! The original point of the popular campaign was to convey the idea that it's good to stop and consider what you are doing and why you are doing it, rather than doing something in haste that you may regret.

I believe that this principle applies today more than ever. Maybe it's time we started displaying bumper stickers that say, "I brake for patience" or "I brake for stillness."

Every day we witness exploding technologies, along with new and improved knowledge at every level. Today's average consumer wears more computer power on his or her wrist, and holds more technology in his or her hand, than existed in the entire world in the early 1960s. We live and work in a radically changing world, and the globalization of our planet means that even more astounding and disruptive changes will be coming our way at breakneck speed—all of which will continue to affect our perception of time and further underscore why we need to stop and think about what we are doing and why we are doing it before charging forward. In the words of Indira Gandhi, "You must learn to be still in the midst of activity and to be vibrantly alive in repose." Gandhi's words resonate and provide sage advice for living in our world today.

> "Learn to get in touch with the silence within yourself and know that everything in this life has a purpose."
> —ELIZABETH KÜBLER-ROSS

Maybe it's time for all of us to just brake for a moment and brace ourselves for (you guessed it) more change. Because in the midst of all the craziness that is going on around us, we can't lose sight of the bigger picture. And what is the bigger picture? It's that for each one of us, life will unfold as it must, and that each of us is a perfect reflection of her or his best self at this moment in time. And timing is everything. Taking action at an inappropriate time just for the sake of taking action serves absolutely no purpose. Sometimes we have to honor the most powerful action of all, stillness and quiet, knowing that it is in this time and space that we find our greatest courage and wisdom.

There's never been a more appropriate time to activate our hearts for greater patience and calmness.

NAVIGATION TOOL: *Activating Your Patient Heart in a High-Speed World*

Take whatever time you need to respond to the following questions. Then assess yourself at the end of this exercise.

> ➤ Describe your level of patience. Do you allow situations in your life to evolve naturally, or do you find yourself, more often than you'd like, forcing things to move forward faster than they should?

➤ Have you experienced a time when forcing things to move more quickly affected the ultimate outcome of a situation? Would the same results have occurred if events had been left to unfold naturally?

_____

_____

➤ Are you able to accept ambiguity, or does ambiguity drive you crazy, causing you to push harder for what you want rather than rely on what will be?

_____

_____

➤ Can you live happily with periods of "not knowing" the outcome of something? Do you wait in joyous expectation of good and anticipation of the answers that will eventually emerge? Or does "not knowing" make you impatient and irritable?

_____

_____

➤ Do you have a patient heart? If you do, describe it. When has it served you well? When do you wish you had activated your patient heart, but didn't?

_____

_____

_____

➤ Do you trust yourself to know when it is appropriate to act and when it is appropriate to wait patiently for the solutions you are seeking?

_____

_____

Self-Assessment

On a scale of 1 to 5, with 5 representing the most patient and 1 representing the least patient, how do you assess your patient heart at this moment in time?

_____

_____

The Impatient Rancher

Late one afternoon, a wealthy rancher asked one of his ranch hands to plant a row of rare trees for his wife's upcoming birthday. The ranch hand said that he would be glad to do so, but he thought his employer should know that trees of this type require a century to grow to full size. "Well, in that case," said the rancher, "gather all the ranch hands; we'd better plant them all this very afternoon."

Sometimes it makes sense to act immediately, and other times, it's better to practice patience.

Forget about Time Management and Learn to Pace Yourself

I don't believe in time management. Time is not something that we can manage. Time is time. There are 24 hours in a day—no more, no less. And herein lies the problem, which is our *perception* of time, not time itself. "Oh, no, time is running out! The clock is ticking. There are not enough hours in the day to do all the things that I must do." When we adopt this attitude toward time, we are letting time rule us and our lives. We become a slave to time, allowing it to dominate us and influence our behaviors so that we fast-forward everything we do, and when we fast-forward life, we miss out on living. We miss out on eating dinner with our kids. We miss out on stopping an extra 2 minutes at the market to buy fresh flowers and appreciate their fragrance once we get them home. We miss out on thousands of little things that we deserve to stop and enjoy.

You may not be able to manage time, but you can certainly live your time more wisely. You can pace yourself, knowing that life is not an all-or-nothing proposition. When you accept this concept of time, the pressures on your life will begin to lift because you will see time in a completely different light and honor it.

Time is no longer the adversary; it becomes fluid, allowing you to pace yourself with ease and better manage your energy.

> "Time is the stuff of which life is made."
> —BENJAMIN FRANKLIN

Here's the bottom line: It's your life. You have the right to establish the tempo and pace at which you live that life. And time? You have all the time you need to realize your dreams and live a life of greater meaning, provided that you use your time wisely and pace yourself along the way.

Time Is a Flexible Navigation Tool

Let time become a flexible life tool in your journey to realizing your higher purpose and greater potential—a crucial navigation instrument that determines your trajectory toward True North and the velocity at which you get there.

Repeat this mantra to yourself when you are feeling that time is not on your side. Copy it and keep it somewhere nearby for quick reference.

> Time is my ally, my buddy. We move through life together in harmony, like best friends. I alone set my life's tempo, and it is the rhythm of my life and how I manage my energy that allows me to fill my time with more love, more interests, and greater meaning.

There are three ways to practice and implement the art of good timing in your life:

➤ Trust the process.

➤ Work with the natural cycles and stages of life.

➤ Thrive on bite-size pieces of small, doable actions.

Trust the Process

When I say "trust the process," I'm referring to the process of our humanity and just being human. Living life means making mistakes—lots of them. It's the process of our higher evolution. We were not born to be ideal, perfect, and without blemishes. Rather, we were born to be real and to be ourselves, not someone else. I love it when right in the middle of a seminar, it suddenly dawns on someone that he doesn't have to live the life that others have told him to live, or when someone suddenly realizes that she no longer has to strive for perfection in her life, and that celebrating humanity is more gratifying than chasing some elusive ideal of perfection that simply does not exist. When this happens, we stop and immediately celebrate our humanity. We do this in class by owning up to our faux pas, laughing out loud from our gut, and accepting a higher good for ourselves.

How often do you celebrate your humanity? Not very often? Then start now. When you celebrate your humanity, you allow yourself to be completely human and authentic to your core, knowing that nothing you do has to be done perfectly and that there is great beauty in the competencies and abilities that you have to offer in this lifetime. When you celebrate your humanity, you also awaken your consciousness to a divine and higher spirit, a spirit that you can trust so that you can let go of your less authentic self.

Perfection is not a requirement of living, yet we strive for perfection whenever we think we can attain it. We push ourselves to be smarter faster and to look younger longer. We even seek our own spirituality in record-breaking time. I call this the "hustle and get spiritual" approach.

I've watched seminar attendees experience a small epiphany when they fully realize that they are not here to be like anyone other than themselves, and that they are here to live life the way only they can live it. This is where trusting the process comes in. Each and every one of us must learn to trust the inner voice of wisdom— the voice that says, "Slow down." "Don't worry about what other people are doing, or what they think about how you are doing what you're doing." "What's the rush?" "Pace yourself."

Just as this chapter's title says, life isn't an all-or-nothing proposition. And being true to your authentic self in a world that does its best to make you conform to something else can be the hardest thing to do. So rather than continue to fight the battle, let go. Surrender yourself to something far more powerful and important, something that will help you to evolve through time and that will guide you, at your own pace, to become what you were meant to be in the time it was meant to happen, for your highest good.

This chapter teaches us to be both eager and patient, and to receive the divine gifts of a greater power. By practicing the art of good timing, we begin to appreciate the cycles and the various stages of our lives.

Work with the Natural Cycles and Stages of Life

In the Hindu tradition, the first third of life is dedicated to a person's education. In the second third, Hindus dedicate themselves to marriage, family, and career. And in the final third, they focus on self-development and spiritual awareness. It is within these three life stages that the Hindus ride the ebb and flow of nature.

I've always thought that this approach made a lot of sense—taking time to thoughtfully and intentionally maximize the most important things in our lives in the natural order in which they present themselves.

Nature's Cycles and How They Affect Us

There are numerous cycles in nature that affect us. The ones that are most commonly referred to are the annual solar cycle of our four seasons, which we will examine last; the monthly lunar cycle; and the 24-hour daily cycle of morning, afternoon, evening, and night. As you navigate your way to True North, it will be imperative that you pay close attention to the cycles of life and how they affect you, both positively and negatively.

"To maintain a powerful pulse in our lives, we must learn how to rhythmically spend and renew energy."
—FROM *THE POWER OF FULL ENGAGEMENT* BY JIM LOEHR AND TONY SCHWARTZ

Nature's Monthly Cycles

Nature's cycles have profound physiological effects on how we feel and how we work, our level of productivity, and our overall energy level and level of creativity. For example, in Judaism, the lunar, not the solar, calendar is used to reflect the cycle of birth to death over a period of 1 year. And not only are the ebb and flow of the ocean's tides affected by lunar cycles—the moon's revolution around the earth—but the blood and fluids of our human bodies are also affected by them. A physician who attended one of my programs told me that she illustrates the powerful effects of monthly lunar cycles to her patients who are facing surgery. "If surgery is not immediately called for," she said, "I will make every attempt to schedule those surgeries that have a greater risk of blood loss during specific parts of the lunar cycle. When this is done, blood loss is known to be significantly less among certain patients and during certain surgical procedures." In this case, the doctor dovetails nature's monthly cycles of ebb and flow with her surgical schedule and, in her opinion, helps to assure a more rapid recovery of her post-op patients.

Without even knowing it, you, too, may have discovered an inclination toward working with nature's cycles. You may have a preferred way of working that enhances your level of productivity and creativity. A good friend of mine, who is also an author, tells me that the greatest bulk of his writing each month takes place between the times of the new moon and the full moon. During the rest of the month, he says, he is much more likely to do the routine administrative tasks that his business requires.

Are you aware of any specific times of the month when you are more productive or creative? Why do you think this is the case? Can you establish a pattern? Try keeping a journal of your most productive and creative times of the month. A month-to-month record will reveal when you are more likely to perform at your peak, or when you exhibit greater creativity and innovative thinking. This information can be quite helpful in planning your work schedule and can significantly increase your productivity when it counts most.

Nature's Daily Cycles

We take this process a step further when we determine the most productive and energetic parts of our day. The Indian Yogis, for example, believe that the spiritual energy of the universe is at its peak when the sun rises and sets. During this daily 24-hour cycle, the Yogis choose to meditate at times that will maximize the full effects of their meditation, believing that this is when the Earth and cosmic energies are in their most delicate balance.

HARMONY AND THE ART OF TIMING THROUGH YOGA AND MEDITATION

As we struggle to keep up with the pace of life, we are surrounded by an ever-increasing number of emotional, mental, and physical ailments: heart conditions in our early thirties, high blood pressure, epidemic proportions of depression, obesity, addiction to drugs and alcohol—and the list goes on. It appears that stress, sedentary lifestyles, and unhealthy diets are the culprits. And so, in this quick-fix world we live in, we often seek quick-fix solutions—crash diets, going on the wagon, attending smoking cessation clinics, and taking a variety of medications—which treat the symptoms, but rarely the cause. The poor results of some of these quick-fix solutions have got us asking, "How much does it all really help in the ultimate analysis?" and "Are these temporary solutions really allowing me to work in harmony with life's natural cycles?" Many of us conclude that maybe it's time we consider a more holistic approach, an approach that has us working in alignment with the cycles of nature—hence the popularity of the practice of Yoga.

What Is Yoga?

The word *Yoga* means "union." Its practice, and the practice of all other forms of spiritual meditation, aims at unifying the human body and mind, with the ultimate goal of reaching a mental state of deep concentration—a higher level of consciousness and a state of harmony between the human mind and a greater universal life force, sometimes considered a spiritual union with the Divine.

The Reality of Meditation and Yoga—It's Not a Perfect World

Yoga and meditation are navigation tools that guide us to our latent sources of inner strength and energy, putting us in harmony with the universe and helping many of us to cope with the daily stresses of living. However, Yoga and meditation are not the keys to a perfect world. That's because there is no such thing. If you use these navigation tools as a way to make your troubles vanish, you will be greatly disappointed. Your children will not magically start earning straight As in school, nor will your manager at work automatically want to pay you more money. In other words, life goes on as always.

However, while some things change and some things stay the same, when you use these powerful life tools to work in sync with the cycles of nature, you will find that you have the ability to better handle what life gives you. You will gain greater insight and sensitivity in dealing with negative emotions, fear, and sadness. You will be learning how to experience these emotions and express them in a healthier fashion, avoiding internal conflict and distress, which often lead to a wide variety of sicknesses and addictions. Practicing the use of tools such as Yoga and other forms of meditation will provide you with a much broader perspective on life's challenges, making it easier for you to handle them with equanimity as you journey toward True North.

I guess you could say that we are following the lead of the Yogis in our quest to find deeper harmony in our lives, as evidenced by the enormous resurgence and popularity of Yoga classes and meditation in general around the world.

NAVIGATION TOOL: *Work with the Flow*

Do you ride the ebb and flow of nature's cycles and life's various stages, or do you fight what feels right in order to do something completely opposite?

You've probably heard the term "go with the flow," an expression that refers to consciously working with the natural flow of things and being in tune with your life's rhythms and the rhythms of others around you. How do you know when you are working with the natural flow of things? You know because it just *feels* right.

Being attuned to what the universe wants and what our True North calls us to be can lead to our riding a wave of unstoppable energy. When this happens, you feel that you are in sync with what's going on around you. When things "feel right," you are more productive, and you perform at your highest levels. Think about what happens when you decide to call someone just because the time *feels* right. More than likely, you have an exhilarating and satisfying conversation. Or think about what happens when you start a project that requires an inordinate amount of hard work and energy, but that's no problem, because you're *feeling* totally in sync with what needs to be done. You tackle the project with unbridled enthusiasm, and you see it through to completion without missing a beat. That's working with the flow. And when you work with the flow, you build momentum. And momentum is essential to perfect timing and to pacing ourselves.

> "To every thing there is a season, and a time to every purpose under the heaven."—ECCLESIASTES 3:1

As a writer, I can tell you that the first 25 pages of a new book I am writing are the hardest pages to write. But once I get those first 25 pages behind me, I've built momentum, and then things just take off and the book starts practically writing itself. When this happens, I know that I am working with the natural flow of nature and that I have tapped a source of energy and forward movement that will help me do my best work. That's what I mean by working with the flow—things that require tremendous effort seem almost effortless.

LIFE COMPASS: *The Four Seasons*

This is a good time to stop and examine the annual solar cycle of the four seasons and relate it to the energy you feel at these different times of the year. Let this exercise be your compass for determining how you can better work with the flow of nature in both your personal and your work life.

Answer following questions for each of the four seasons.

How can you best align your temperament and tempo with this season so that you remain consistently working with the flow? Describe how being attuned to this season helps you in your quest to discover your True North. How does the rhythm of your life change during this particular season? How does this rhythm affect your productivity and performance on the job? How does it affect your personal relationships and your home life? How does the change of seasons allow you to pace yourself, freeing you from anxiety and stress? Is there one season more than another in which you feel your best self emerge?

Nature's Powerful Annual Cycle: The Four Seasons

Spring

Spring is a time when new beginnings and fresh starts come to mind. There is a great deal of energy in the spring. You can feel it. And some of that energy is strong and overcomes resistance, like seeds breaking through winter soil to create new life. Springtime is about giving birth to new ideas and concepts. It is a time of fertility and creation. Spring offers us new energy for new beginnings.

Journal your responses to the earlier questions here.

_____

_____

_____

_____

_____

Summer

Summer marks a time of great abundance. It's when crops grow and flowers bloom and flourish. It takes a great deal of energy to get things going in the spring, and summer uses that momentum to continue what has been started. Summer is often a time of great success and accomplishment. Nature accomplishes a great deal in a short time during the summer months, and so do we. In the summer our productivity and performance soar.

Journal your responses to the earlier questions here.

_____

_____

_____

_____

Autumn

Autumn is a time for reaping what we have sown. It also is a time of assessment and celebration, of thankfulness and abundance. We separate the wheat from the chaff in the fall. We often do the same in our personal and work relationships, evaluating what works for us and what projects or people we must eliminate because they are not in alignment with our goals and objectives, principles, and values. Productivity and performance start to wind down in the fall.

Journal your responses to the earlier questions here.

_____

_____

_____

_____

_____

Winter

Winter is considered a time of deep reflection and silence. It is during this time of reflection and quiet that thoughts deep within our unconscious mind come to the surface of our conscious mind. Winter is also a time of cocooning and protecting ourselves from the outside elements. Productivity and performance are usually lower in winter, and more rest and deeper thought are required.

Journal your responses to the earlier questions here.

_____

_____

_____

_____

_____

Manifest Your Gifts—Examine the Patterns of Nature

When we examine the patterns of nature (see Figure 6-1), we are drawn to examine our own natural patterns, as you have just done. Now let's go a step further. Do you demonstrate cyclical patterns of recurring behaviors? Would you say that these behaviors are life-enhancing and positive, or are they negative, sometimes holding you back from doing your best? For example, suppose something happens to you one time. Let's say you miss a deadline at work because of unforeseen circumstances that held up the project along the way. You can probably say that this is a one-time, rare occurrence. But suppose you routinely miss deadlines at work. Let's say that you miss deadlines so frequently that your colleagues predict that you will do so. This is quite a different matter.

There are certain predictable patterns of behavior that we cannot consider to be rare occurrences or accidents. Instead, they are behaviors and occurrences for which we are fully responsible and accountable, and they are possibly indicative of

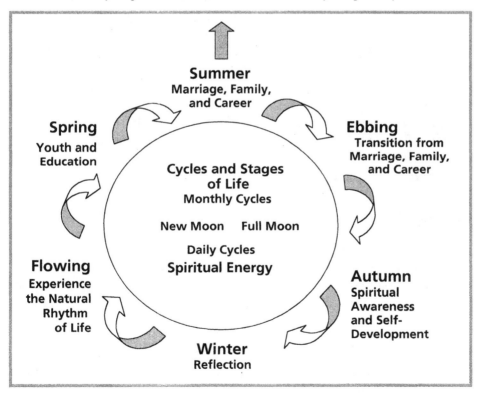

Figure 6-1. Working with the Natural Cycles and Stages of Life

destructive patterns. When destructive patterns emerge around us, we may find ourselves in a cycle of self-sabotage. By acknowledging that this is happening to us, we are able to do something about it and to examine what is working and what is not working in our lives. When we do this, we give ourselves the opportunity to create new patterns of behavior—patterns that will help us to move in harmony with the natural cycles and stages of life. When we move in sync with the universe, we can fully celebrate our humanity and manifest our gifts and greater potential.

Thrive on Bite-Size Pieces of Small, Doable Actions

In this chapter we have focused on the importance of practicing good timing and pacing ourselves. You don't have to do everything all at once, but you do need to do something. The trick is to establish a gentle flow of ideas that will keep you moving forward. By connecting with the natural flow of the universe and the cycles of nature, you are doing this very thing. And when you learn to pace yourself this way, you keep yourself from getting overwhelmed by a flood of activities and thoughts that often create greater pressure and tension, because you're not moving forward and releasing that pent-up energy.

Is it any wonder that we sometimes feel taut and stretched beyond our capacity? For all of us, there's got to be a steady release in our lives—a reliable way of letting the pressures and energies out.

Pacing ourselves and our lives is about moving the energy out of us in a slow and steady flow. As author Julia Cameron says, "Easy does it, because the truth is, easy does do it, and frantic, forced, and frenetic does not." I consider her words pearls of wisdom when it comes to practicing the art of good timing in our lives.

Time Flies When You're in the Present

We thrive when we move through life in small, bite-size pieces of doable actions, savoring every bit of where we are at this moment in time—the present. When we do this, we set ourselves up for success, rather than failure. We give ourselves room to create forward motion on our ideas and act on our greatest dreams and passions.

Moving into Your Equilibrium: Week 2 Review

Nice going! You have completed the exercises in the chapters for Week 2 of the Discover True North program:

➤ Recognize and Activate Your Inner Voice of Wisdom and Courage

➤ Cultivate Interests before Callings

➤ Pace Yourself—Life Isn't an All-or-Nothing Proposition

Go back and review all three chapters' lessons and exercises and use the following four steps to reflect on what you learned in Week 2. Allow these four steps to help move you toward your equilibrium for higher learning and understanding. Think about how you have been able to improve your life using one section of this book at a time. How will you apply and practice each chapter's higher purpose statement in your own life?

STEP 1: *Stop and Breathe*

As you begin, clear your mind and reflect on the key points of Week 2 and what you've learned. Start by taking some deep breaths and slowly releasing them. Relax and consider how the lessons you have gleaned from these chapters might enhance or enlighten your life. Jot down ways in which you feel more confident or inspired. Fully appreciate the new or higher perspectives that you may have gained from this week's lessons, and focus on what matters most.

STEP 2: *Be Conscious and Think*

How has what you have learned this week served to raise your consciousness to a higher level? How will you benefit from your raised consciousness? List some of the ways in which you will activate your awareness levels. Write down what you know to be most important at this time and place in your life. How do you plan to maintain your focus and your attention to the details?

STEP 3: *Choose and Commit*

What life choices will you make and commit to carrying through after completing this week's lessons? In what ways do you anticipate that your choices will move you to a newer, stronger inner wisdom? Give examples of how you will avoid taking a path of least resistance when you are faced with a challenge. What moments from this week's lessons represent your deepest truths? Describe the ways in which you demonstrate these truths on a daily basis.

STEP 4: *Act and Then Move toward Something*

How will you take action on what you've learned this week? List specific steps that you will take that will move you toward your higher purpose. How have the lessons this week guided you closer to your True North? What will you need to review and work on for ongoing improvement and personal development? What schedule will you set to accomplish this?

After completing these four steps, you are now ready to move on to Week 3: "Connecting with Your Spirit without Disconnecting from Your Brain."

WEEK
3

Connecting with Your Spirit without Disconnecting from Your Brain

7

Live Your Fullest Multisensory Life

Higher Purpose Statement

We are not simply human beings who are on a path to fulfillment and higher purpose. We are multisensory beings who are on a human path of discovery. To see yourself simply as someone who is on an inspirational journey of greater purpose would be to minimize all of the magnificent inner strength and authentic power that you hold within you. You have the power to live your fullest multisensory life, a life richer than the one that your five senses alone can provide. Multisensory is not better than five-sensory. It is simply a more advanced compass, or life tool, of your inner guidance system. It is in the unity of both your multisensory abilities and your five-sensory abilities that you will experience the upward spiral of your fullest potential.

Two Schools of Seeking Higher Purpose

Since you have come this far in the program, it's a good bet that you are someone who is seeking to connect with her or his spirit or higher self without disconnecting from your brain or your individual way of thinking. Until recent years, there have typically been two schools of thought when it comes to seeking higher purpose and greater life meaning. One focuses on a nonphysical world, often thought of as higher consciousness, soul, or spirit; and the other focuses on a physical world, the intellectual realm of more scientifically based theories and facts. I believe that if we are to live life with the greatest of reverence, we must honor both our physical being—mind and body—and our spirit. When we allow this to happen, we become the best we can be and reach our highest potential; we experience authentic joy and inner peace (see Figure 7-1).

Reverence of Mind and Spirit

=

Highest Potential, Authentic Joy, and Inner Piece

Figure 7-1. Reverence of Mind and Spirit

Your Brain Is the Container; Your Spirit Is the Process

Your brain is the "container" that holds your intellect and all of your other intelligences and competencies, which we discussed back in Chapter 3. Within this container is the ability to make decisions and life choices. It is the place from which you decide to act on your intentions and choose whether or not to move forward toward True North, determining what you will do and how you will behave and treat others along the way. It is your mind that shapes your choices and helps you decide how to apply your natural gifts and competencies at certain times and places in your life. It also can, as the word suggests, sometimes contain or restrict you—as when you procrastinate over something or analyze things for a prolonged period of time.

> "An integral being knows without going, sees without looking, and accomplishes without doing."—LAO TZU

It is within this container that our minds bring forth our most creative genius, ideas, and discoveries—cures for diseases, Pulitzer Prize–winning novels, memorable symphonies, and beautiful art—all of which begin in the mind as a single thought. This container is your personality, your conscious self, and your five physical senses—seeing, hearing, touching, smelling, and tasting.

Spirit, on the other hand, is not something that we can see, hear, touch, smell, or taste. It is our nonphysical being. Think of your nonphysical being as a spiraling *process* that circles upward—a process that starts from deep within you and extends far above and beyond your five senses to a higher level of multisensory intuition and greater potential. It is the most private and sacred connection between you and your unconscious wisdom, intuition, and God (bearing in mind that what is here referred to as God is known by different names in different world traditions).

Connecting with your spirit without disconnecting from your brain requires building a bridge of deeper understanding between traditional and nontraditional practices when it comes to seeking your higher self. These are practices that bridge the gap between mind and spirit.

It is through honoring both your mind and your spirit that you will be lifted to a higher state of conscious living, intuitive purpose, and greater potential (see Figure 7-2). This is what is called becoming a multisensory person.

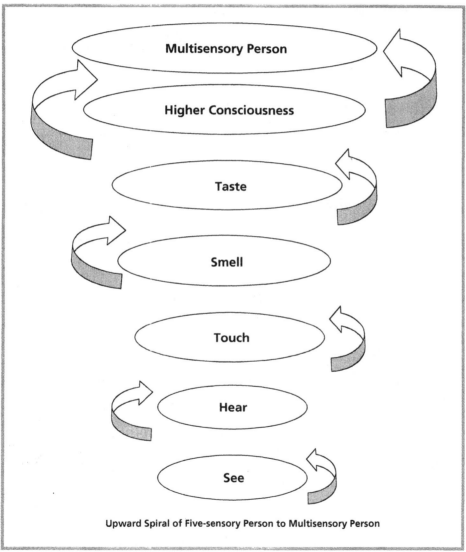

Multisensory Person

Higher Consciousness

Taste

Smell

Touch

Hear

See

Upward Spiral of Five-sensory Person to Multisensory Person

Figure 7-2. Higher Self—Greater Potential, Authenticity, and Purpose

The Multisensory Person Combines Intellect and Faith

When you become multisensory, you find that using your intellect and faith in tandem is a natural action that will help you in staying the course toward True North.

Multisensory people learn to trust their intelligence and their innate ability to reason, and then they let that reinforce the higher sense of wisdom, along with the flexibility to adjust and set new goals and destinations along life's journey. Multisensory people maintain their faith, knowing that believing in something greater than themselves will always guide them through life's uncharted and sometimes turbulent waters.

The Evolution Has Begun

Earlier in this book, I talked about the evolutionary transformation that is taking place within our collective humanity—an evolution in which people in record numbers are seeking higher consciousness, greater meaning, and authentic power in their lives. Getting there, however, requires sharper and more updated tools and techniques for navigating the best course.

In Chapter 8, I will address the importance of the way in which True North directs us closer to our authentic power—where our soul and our personality come into alignment, bringing forth our greatest gifts and competencies—and at the same time moves us away from our external power—appearances, job titles, material possessions, money, and control. For now, just know that discovering your authentic power is an important part of becoming a multisensory individual.

Exchanging Limitations for Greater, More Powerful Opportunity

The human race is evolving from being five-sensory to being multisensory. Together, our five senses—sight, hearing, touch, smell, and taste—form a single sensory system that is set up to help us perceive our physical reality. However, simply perceiving and appreciating our physical reality isn't going to be enough if we are intent on connecting with our spirit or higher self.

This isn't to say that being multisensory is better than being five sensory. It is not. But as we evolve to higher levels of consciousness, it is easier to make comparisons between a system that has greater limitations and one that offers greater opportunity and insight. The life of a multisensory person is filled with more opportunities for both personal and professional growth and development. We are evolving to become more multisensory, just as we once evolved from using horses and buggies to driving cars, or from burning candles for light to using electricity. Our multisensory evolution is the natural step upward to becoming all that we are meant to be.

Learning from the Greatest Teachers

All of our great teachers are, or have been, multisensory individuals. Take Albert Einstein, for example. Today, many consider him a mystic as well as a physicist. Like so many other scientists, Einstein did not rely on the limitations of his five senses, nor did he rely on answers in three-dimensional reality. While in the process of discovering the theory of relativity, Einstein said that he did so by *seeing* himself traveling on a beam of light. Referring to the power of mystical awe, Einstein once said, "The most beautiful thing we can experience is the mysterious. It is the source of all true art and science."

I, for one, believe that Einstein was a great mystic, although I highly doubt that Einstein himself would have used that term, or that Carl Jung or William James would have done so. This is only because back then there was a great stigma attached to anyone who did not conform and work strictly within the accepted scientific models. But I do not for one second believe that deep down, within their authentic selves, these men were ever limited by their five senses, and, as a result, their works and their multisensory skills contributed to the evolutionary transformation of the world we live in today. It is from the perspective of this mystical or invisible higher realm that the power and compassionate acts of someone like Gandhi become explicable and even more profound.

I think that teachers like Gandhi understood long ago the importance of being able to connect with their spirit without disconnecting from their mind and that they blended their mind and their soul to reach an extraordinary place of intuition and inspiration before it became acceptable to do so. Obviously Einstein and Gandhi clearly knew that there was more than the realm of time, space, and matter—something more than just the five senses of our physical life—and they, like some others, successfully tapped into it.

How can you, too, cultivate the qualities of a multisensory person? Granted, these abilities come more naturally to some than to others, but all of us have within us the power to develop our higher sense of intuition, or gut hunches.

"There is a universal intelligent life force that exists within everyone and everything. It resides within each one of us as a deep wisdom, an inner knowing. We can access this wonderful source of knowledge and wisdom through our intuition: an inner sense that tells us what feels right and true for us at any given moment."
—SHAKTI GAWAIN

Using the following Life Compass, begin exploring some of the ways in which you will sharpen your intuitive talents and multisensory gifts.

LIFE COMPASS: *Suggestions and Exercises for Becoming a Multisensory Person*

➤ Read about mystical and multisensory people like Einstein, Deepak Chopra, Saint Teresa of Avila, Gandhi, Mohammed, Benjamin Lee, Lee Whorf, Jesus, Shakti Gawain, and Nikola Tesla. Intuition and multisensory talents rub off. What people do you know who are multisensory or extremely intuitive? Add their names to this list here:

_____

_____

_____

➤ What is it about these people that, in your opinion, makes them intuitive, mystical, or multisensory? What examples portray their use of more than just their five senses?

_____

_____

_____

➤ Investigate different types of meditation. Most meditation techniques have one thing in common: They calm the mind and soothe the soul. The Christian mystic St. John of the Cross said, "The key to union with the soul is silence and work. Work we have; it's silence where God and the soul's voice can more easily be heard." There are many different kinds of meditation. Take the time to look into several types and select one that works for you. Meditation does not have to be lengthy or complicated in order to work. It doesn't require a house full of burning candles, an altar, or your own personal shaman. I know people who meditate for a few minutes each day at work, or in the bathtub, or while waiting in line at the grocery store, or while riding the subway to work. Do whatever works for you. There are no right or wrong ways to engage in a multisensory life.

➤ Respond to the following: Do you meditate? If you do, what are your meditation practices? What other meaningful practices would you like to incorporate into what you are doing now? Does meditating help you to achieve higher awareness and peace of mind? If you do not meditate, what is stopping you? How can you overcome this obstacle?

_____

_____

_____

_____

➤ Experience the power of prayer. Prayer and meditation are not the same. In prayer, our personality communicates messages to a higher power, saying those things that we would like it to know. In meditation, we are on the receiving end of the messages. Both are powerful ways for connecting your spirit with your brain. Prayer, like meditation, can be very simple. Just saying "thank you" is a simple way of praying that brings you closer to appreciating more of what you have, rather than focusing on what you don't have or wish you had. The multisensory aspects of prayer have proved enormously effective for many who claim that their prayers have been not only heard, but answered in a multitude of ways.

➤ Respond to the following if appropriate. What experiences have you had with prayer? How do you think prayer builds a bridge between your five senses and your higher-level senses? What would be the objective, or benefits, of having prayer and meditation work in tandem?

_____

_____

_____

➤ Choose a soulful hobby. Join a Yoga class, buy a season ticket to the symphony, start a garden, take a photography class or a sailing class, take flying lessons, try surfing or fly fishing, read poetry. All of these things can bring you closer to developing multisensory perceptions. Hobbies like these will help you to uncover what inspires you most and brings forth a higher level of consciousness and understanding for managing life's greatest challenges.

➤ What other soulful practices and hobbies can you add to this list that would sharply focus your inspiration and insights?

_____

_____

_____

_____

_____

➤ Read the books *Intuition: The Path to Inner Wisdom,* by Patricia Einstein, and *Developing Intuition: Practical Guidance for Daily Life,* by Shakti Gawain. In these books, you will find step-by-step exercises and guidance for mind, body, and spirit. When you take the time to develop your intuition, you will better connect with the guiding force in your life, your True North.

➤ Become committed to developing your intuitive abilities. Allow your intuition to appear naturally whenever possible. In other words, don't fight it or talk yourself out of it. Follow up on hunches; pay close attention to that tiny voice inside you that tells you *not* to go there tonight. Let your intuition serve you as a survival and protective mechanism. Let it become a walkie-talkie between you and the Divine. As a writer, I can tell you that there have been many times when I was in a deep fog of confusion and writer's block, and I received precisely the inspiration and answers I was looking for. And beyond that, when I allowed that divine presence to assist me, it has actually worked through me in formulating chapters and outlines for books and creating numerous training workshops and leader's guides, almost as if I'd had a coauthor sitting by my side. I believe that intentionally sharpening my multisensory skills has allowed me to spiral upward and tap a more profound and knowledgeable source.

➤ Now it's your turn to describe a time when you felt a "knowingness" about something. How did this come to you, and how did you feel when it did?

_____

_____

_____

_____

➤ Whatever the experiences you have described in this exercise may be, you should know that these are, at some level, multisensory experiences and that you are a multisensory person.

Next, I want you to start a multisensory journal or notebook. In this journal, I want you to keep track of your multisensory or intuitive experiences and insights. The more you pay attention to these occurrences, the more attuned and awakened you will be to your higher self, and the more you will be able to live your fullest multisensory life.

Where Spirit and Intellect Converge

I like to think of the spiritual journey that we take and the intellectual journey that we take as two great rivers that converge, both flowing in the same direction of higher consciousness—a consciousness that can be achieved without separating, or disconnecting, one from the other. This consciousness is so powerful that it evokes guidance to a path of higher purpose and meaning—our True North.

Your Inner Guidance System and Your True North Are Always with You

At the beginning of this book, we talked about the many questions that probably fill your mind—questions like "What is my greater purpose?" "What do I have to contribute to this organization that will have lasting meaning?" "How will I know when I reach my greatest potential?" "What can I do to reignite my passion?"

In the process of seeking answers to these and other questions, you have been moving forward, day by day, week by week, in this program, Discover True North. You have been completing exercises and reevaluating and assessing your inner strengths and challenges. By this time, in Week 3 of the program, you may even be feeling some invisible force or form of guidance moving within you, taking your hand, and leading you in a certain direction—the direction of your True North. What I want you to realize is that both this inner guidance system and your True North were with you long before you picked up this book and starting reading.

Maybe there have been times when you've been caught up in the moment of life and failed to recognize the authenticity and internal power of your inner guidance system. But stop for a moment and glance back over the years. I bet you can recall several instances when an invisible strength and inner power has guided you when you needed it most. Perhaps this invisible force challenged you, inspired you, or brought you successfully through a specific time of crisis and sadness. Perhaps these were all times when you felt you had lost your way.

If You've Fallen Away from Your Path, Just Get Back On

Maybe you're reading this book because you believe that, for some reason, you have missed certain windows of opportunity in your life, and you are worried that they may never again present themselves. Maybe you chose to go against the invisible forces calling to you. Or maybe you were too young and immature, or too wrapped up in material possessions and your quest for external power, to just let go and be true to yourself and your greater calling. I'm here to tell you that none of that matters now. Because this is the great gift of True North: No matter how or when you may have lost your way, when you embrace both intellect and faith, connecting with your spirit without disconnecting from your brain, as this chapter's title says, True North will present itself once again—a reliable fixed point in the heavens, and as bright as ever to guide you home.

8

The Four Declarations of Your Authentic Power

Higher Purpose Statement

Authentic power makes you happy to be alive. It is your truest self. It is a good thing—a really good thing. And when you have it, you never compare yourself to anyone else or feel the need to impress people. Your authentic power is the opposite of your external power. External power comes only from *what* you are doing at the moment, and that kind of power is never permanent. It comes and goes. Authentic power comes from *how* you are doing what you are *supposed* to be doing. Authentic power always feels right and is fulfilling. When you are filled with authentic power, you are confident and free of doubt. You are happy, and you look forward to each new day. Your authentic power can be felt and experienced anywhere, at any time—at home, at work, at the gym, at a party, on an African safari, or anywhere else. Authentic power is boundless.

Authentic Power—When Your Truest Self and Your Soul Align

Ralph Waldo Emerson wrote, "What lies behind us and what lies ahead of us are tiny matters compared to what lies within us." I believe that what lies within us is all that we can become, all that we stand for, and all that we believe—our authentic selves. And it is the alignment of our personality with our soul's desire that gives us our authentic power (see Figure 8-1). Think of it this way: Your soul, or maybe you'd like to call it your inner being, knows your life's greater purpose and what you are meant to do in this world. But it is your personality that has the gifts, competencies, and talents to achieve this. When the two come together in perfect synchronization, you have what is called a *soul-connected personality*—an expression I use and illustrate in my workshops, which implies that we are neither purely physical beings nor purely soul beings. We are both.

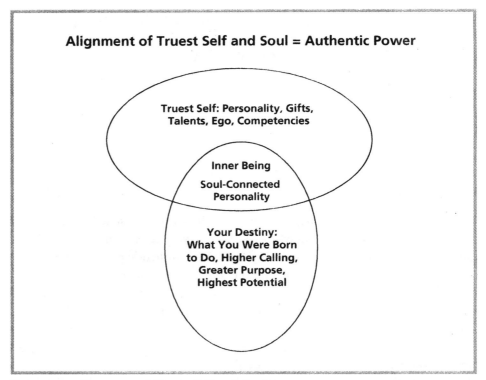

Alignment of Truest Self and Soul = Authentic Power

Truest Self: Personality, Gifts, Talents, Ego, Competencies

Inner Being

Soul-Connected Personality

Your Destiny: What You Were Born to Do, Higher Calling, Greater Purpose, Highest Potential

Figure 8-1. Alignment of Truest Self and Soul

When a person's personality and ego take over and are separated from the person's soul, the soul begins to starve. In my workshops I often refer to Dr. Thomas Moore's book, *Care of the Soul*, and what he calls a "loss of soul" in our world—a malady that when neglected manifests itself in despair, depression, hopelessness, and feelings of emptiness. I believe it is this "loss of soul" that triggers so much unhappiness and doubt in people's lives. When I am asked to illustrate this, I point to a distinct detachment between both entities, the space between that conveys the gap we must work to close if we are to discover True North (see Figure 8-2).

And by the same token, when a person's soul is separated from his or her truest self, that person will be incapable of reaching his or her highest potential, true call-

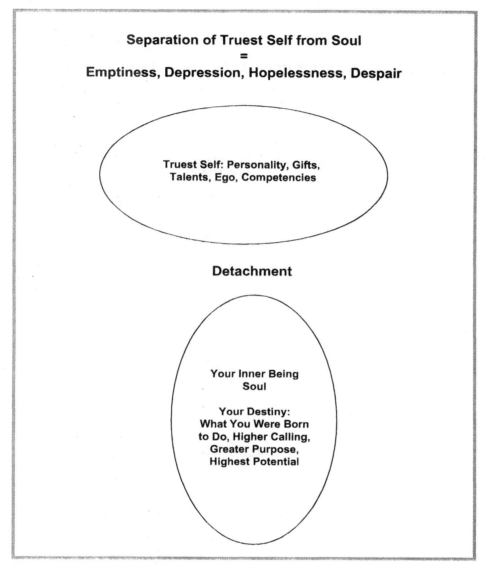

Separation of Truest Self from Soul
=
Emptiness, Depression, Hopelessness, Despair

Truest Self: Personality, Gifts,
Talents, Ego, Competencies

Detachment

Your Inner Being
Soul

Your Destiny:
What You Were Born
to Do, Higher Calling,
Greater Purpose,
Highest Potential

Figure 8-2. Separation of Truest Self from Soul

ing, or destiny. Why? Because there must be a physical vessel through which the soul and personality can connect and work in tandem to prosper and flourish, thrive and grow, setting the stage for each of us to become all that she or he was meant to be in this lifetime (see Figure 8-3).

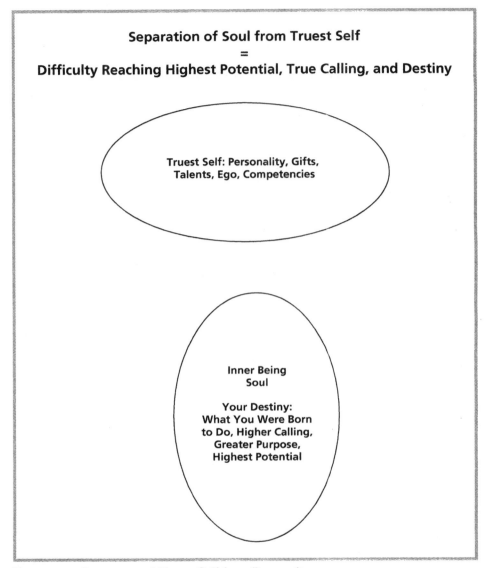

Separation of Soul from Truest Self

=

Difficulty Reaching Highest Potential, True Calling, and Destiny

Truest Self: Personality, Gifts, Talents, Ego, Competencies

**Inner Being
Soul**

**Your Destiny:
What You Were Born
to Do, Higher Calling,
Greater Purpose,
Highest Potential**

Figure 8-3. Separation of Truest Self from Personality

Authentic Power Helps Us Co-Create a Better World

Your True North is the magnetic force that is tugging at you right now, gently guiding you into alignment of your soul and your personality. It is when this alignment occurs that the authentic power that you were born to have and use becomes real.

Authentic power helps us all to become co-creators of greater good in the world.

Your authentic power is mighty. When you achieve your authentic power, you will be able to give all that you were born to give, and you will receive all that the universe has to offer you. Authentic power is the human experience without the human foibles.

Attaining and maintaining your authentic power is a lifetime endeavor that requires your total commitment. In their book *The Heart of the Soul,* Gary Zukav and Linda Francis state that an authentically empowered person is someone who is in partnership with the universe. And the more a person develops that partnership, the more authentically empowered that person's life becomes. I happen to agree with their philosophy, and I also believe that as students of this earth, we are all taking the same course in trying to develop our authentic power. Here is a process that I use to guide my students as they take the necessary steps to declare their authentic power. The process involves what I call the four declarations of your authentic power, and it requires serious commitment to the following actions:

> **"Be what you are. This is the first step toward becoming better than you are."**
> —J. C. HARE AND A. W. HARE, BRITISH CLERICS AND WRITERS

Step 1: Declare what matters most to you.

Step 2: Declare what is important today.

Step 3: Declare your sacred soul impressions.

Step 4: Declare your authentic self.

Step 1: Declare What Matters Most to You

In order to experience your authentic power, you have to know what matters most to you. What genuinely motivates you to be your best and to do your best work? By taking time to assess what's most important to you, your work ethic, your principles, and your highest standards, you can better determine what drives you in a positive direction.

LIFE COMPASS: *Personal Motivation Diagnostic*

On a scale of 1 to 4, with 4 being the highest rating and 1 being the lowest, rate each of the following motivators and circle the number that best reflects the degree to which this matters to you and motivates you to be your best, most authentic, and most powerful self.

1. People showing concern for me as a person	4	3	2	1
2. Good working relationships with others	4	3	2	1
3. Feeling empowered and trusted	4	3	2	1
4. Faith in a higher power, i.e., God, Spirit, Divine, Buddha, True Light, Jesus, etc.	4	3	2	1
5. Closeness with family and friends	4	3	2	1
6. Recognition of my efforts	4	3	2	1
7. Delegation of responsibility to me	4	3	2	1
8. Being promoted	4	3	2	1
9. Close contact with family, friends, and coworkers	4	3	2	1
10. Making lots of money	4	3	2	1
11. Getting along with others	4	3	2	1
12. Honest praise	4	3	2	1
13. Constructive and helpful feedback	4	3	2	1
14. Coaching when I need it	4	3	2	1
15. The satisfaction of a job well done	4	3	2	1
16. Being included in social functions	4	3	2	1
17. Knowing what people expect of me; being given clear objectives	4	3	2	1
18. Job security	4	3	2	1

Now that you have determined your most important and least important personal motivators, narrow down the list. Look only at the selections you rated 4 and choose your top three motivators. By doing this, you are declaring your most important personal motivators—what sets you on fire and keeps you going with all that you've got. Knowing this is part of understanding your authentic power.

I may not know you personally, but I can tell you that this diagnostic consistently generates similar results. For example, people rarely, if ever, rank statement 10 (making lots of money) as their highest priority or personal driving force. Sure, money is a motivating factor in our lives, but it is not what matters most for the majority of folks. And although compensation can give some people external power, it can never give someone authentic power. The selections in the assessment that typically rate highest are statements 1, 2, 4, 5, 6, 12, and 15.

Declare what matters most to you by writing your response here.

I Declare That What Matters Most to Me Is

_____

This navigation tool can be very powerful in the workplace as well. Using the same format, and eliminating any sensitive statements concerning workplace behavior, ask those with whom you work to assess themselves. What might their responses tell you about them? For starters, just asking someone to share with you what matters to her or him makes that person feel appreciated and listened to. It sends a message that says, "I care about what you think and how you feel about what matters most." This is a tool that can greatly improve communication, both at home and on the job.

Like your authentic power, motivation is intrinsic, meaning that it comes from within. When you take time to really think about and declare what matters most to you and what motivates you to be your best and to co-create a better world, you are moving closer to True North and experiencing your authentic power.

Step 2: Declare What Is Important Today

Your authentic power can be effective only if you are living in the moment. Right here, right now is all that you have. Stop thinking about the past and worrying about the future. It's wasted energy.

> "All you really need to do is accept this moment fully. You are then at ease in the here and now and at ease with yourself."—ECKHART TOLLE, FROM *PRACTICING THE POWER OF NOW*, A COMPANION BOOK TO *THE POWER OF NOW*

All you really need to do is accept this moment fully. You are then at ease in the here and now and at ease with yourself.

Therefore, I am inviting you to figure out what is really important in your life over the next 24 hours. This exercise is a Life Compass that will help you to uncover what is truly important in the big picture of your life, what you value most, and what you know deep down in your core to be true and authentic. It takes the previous declaration that you completed about *what matters most to you* a step further by helping you to focus on just the here and now.

LIFE COMPASS: *My Last 24 Hours on Earth*

I want you to imagine what it would be like if you knew for certain that you only had 24 hours left to live on this earth. Pretend that tomorrow at this same time, your life as you know it will come to an end. Contemplate what you would do if you had just one day.

Now sit down at your computer, or take a pen and paper, and begin to figure out the things that are most important to you at this very moment in time. Remember, you have only the next 24 hours left. Responding to the following questions will help you get started.

➤ What is one thing in your life that you have always wanted to do, but haven't gotten around to doing?

➤ If you could make one wish (other than living beyond the next 24 hours), what would you wish for? Would the wish be for yourself or for someone else, and how would you try to make it come true in one day?

➤ When was the last time you spoke to your family and friends and told them you loved them? When did you last tell these people how much you admire them or respect their accomplishments?

➤ Is there someone in your family, or perhaps a friend, to whom you are no longer speaking because of a disagreement? Would you like to make amends before your 24 hours are up? If so, what would you say?

➤ How many important things in your life do you have dangling out there unfinished that should have been taken care of long ago? Maybe it's a living trust you've been meaning to get around to finishing, taking your 90-year-old grandfather out to dinner, or calling your oldest, dearest friend and telling her how much you appreciate her for always being there for you.

Now add to this list of responses any additional things going on in your life that you'd like to have wrapped up before your 24 hours are over.

Next, answer the following question: What do you plan to do about this unfinished business? How will you take action on the things on this list so that your last day on earth is the best it can be?

When completed, this exercise will reveal your life's most important unfinished issues and will pose the questions, "What are you doing about them? What actions are you taking to make today your best day on this earth? Because today is all that any of us have.

When I suggested this exercise in one of my seminars, a few people thought it a bit dramatic, and some even thought it unnecessary. Then September 11, 2001, happened, and I got dozens of emails from people who had attended the seminar saying thank you and saying that they were now taking the exercise seriously and planned to use it as an ongoing Life Compass.

Sometimes it takes something drastic or even tragic to open our eyes to the fact that life is short and that we should never put off to tomorrow what we can take care of today. What are you putting off that you could do today? What would make your "now" on this earth the best it can be?

Declare what is important to you today by writing your response here.

I Declare These Things to Be Most Important to Me Today

Step 3: *Declare Your Sacred Soul Impressions*

Your authentic power is a compelling tool that gives you the ability to elevate and change your life. It is in the sacred presence of your inner being, infused with your personality and talents, that your authentic self meets your authentic power, and it is from your authentic power that you create the soul or life impressions that you leave to others.

> "I wish that life should not be cheap, but sacred."
> —RALPH WALDO EMERSON

You may be overlooking one of the most important and precious gifts that you have to offer. I call this gift our soul impressions. Soul impressions are born from our authentic selves and help us to build our authentic power. They are not impressions or gifts that come from ego or things, like the car you drive, your job title, your public status, or trophies that you may have won. Your soul impressions include everything that is authentically you, like your individual beauty, your weaknesses, your dreams, your successes, and your failures. They include your earliest childhood memories, whom you married, and whom you didn't marry. They include your fears and your frailties, your most magnificent talents and your grandest life yearnings. All of these things and more make up the essence of who you are and leave behind your soul impressions.

LIFE COMPASS: *My Sacred Soul Impressions*

Your soul impressions are valuable gifts that you can share with others or simply cherish for yourself. Soul impressions help us to appreciate the essence of who we are and what we have lived through. They are life compasses that help guide us toward our deepest desires and our True North.

This mix of life and soul impressions comes together when you accumulate your most meaningful mementos, those that tell the story of your life. How do you do this? Start by getting a container or a box. It can be a plain shoebox, a floral-covered box, a hatbox, or just a cardboard box that you have decorated any way you like.

Now select the 12 items that matter most to you. Think of your container or box as a personal treasure chest that will hold all of the significance and treasures of your life. Next, hunt for these treasures. By searching your house, your parents' house, and other places, you will actually begin the process of seeking out the unique, one-of-a-kind treasures of your soul. Search high and low until you find the 12 items that are of most significance to you.

Here are some suggestions for what goes into your soul impressions treasure chest:

- A piece of jewelry

- Love letters

- Heirlooms

- Photographs

- Coins

- A pressed flower

- An article of clothing

- A seashell

- A newspaper clipping

- A piece of cloth

- A lock of hair

- An old car key or house key

If an item is too big to fit in your container, write the name of it on a slip of paper or draw a picture of it.

How will you use your soul impressions after you've collected everything? First, put the box away somewhere safe. Wait a few weeks, and then, on a rainy

Saturday afternoon or a lazy Sunday morning, get a cup of tea or coffee, take out your soul impressions box, sit down, and go through it, one piece at a time. If you feel comfortable doing so, share your items with a close friend or relative, someone who is important to you.

Like snowflakes, your soul impressions represent your unique and most authentic self. But unlike snowflakes, your soul impressions will never melt. They will remain a vivid part of your personal legacy.

Declare your sacred soul impressions by writing your response here.

I Declare that My Sacred Soul Impressions Include

Step 4: Declare Your Authentic Self

Getting to your authentic self is sometimes easier than maintaining your authenticity. That takes a lot of work. Maintaining your authenticity is something that comes from within you, not outside of you. You can't just go get it. Nor can you meditate your way to it or wish it to happen. Your authentic self is made up of all your intentions and life choices. And by choosing your intentions and making certain life choices, you are declaring your authenticity to the world and to your higher self. This is also important to the process of claiming your authentic power.

> **"Swear an oath to authenticity."—RABBI MARC GAFNI, AUTHOR OF *SOUL PRINTS***

Maybe you've heard the term *ethical will*. This is actually a biblical custom handed down through the centuries. You are asked to write an ethical will giving your intentions, beliefs, wisdom, and life practices. An ethical will contains the principles and values you have practiced in your life that you would like to leave to future generations. Writing an ethical will plays an important role in declaring your authentic self.

LIFE COMPASS: *My Ethical Will of Intentions and Beliefs*

Now I would like you to write your ethical will of intentions and beliefs to your children. If you don't have children, write it to your godchildren, your nieces or nephews, or your friends' children.

In your ethical will, I want you to list all the pearls of wisdom that you have gathered throughout your lifetime. One of my students wrote that after having suffered the health scare of her life, breast cancer, she came to the realization that such scares can really be life's greatest gifts in disguise. The cancer caused her to stop and reevaluate her stressful life and job. As a result, she learned how to design a new life for herself, a life of peaceful rituals and serenity. She survived the cancer and continues to practice inner peace and joy on a daily basis.

Write down in your ethical will things that you believe to be true or know for sure in your heart. One gentleman from my workshop wrote, "Stand for something, or you will fall for anything."

State the intentions and beliefs you had by living the life you've lived. Record the values and principles by which you have conducted yourself.

> "You die when you are faking it, and you are alive when you are truthful."
> —MARIA IREN FORNES, CUBAN-AMERICAN PLAYWRIGHT

My Ethical Will of Intentions and Beliefs

_____   _____

_____   _____

_____   _____

_____   _____

_____   _____

_____   _____

_____   _____

Declare your authentic self by writing your response here.

I Declare My Authentic Self to Be

_____   _____

When you assign action to the four declarations of your authentic power, you are declaring that you are true to yourself and that you are now ready to elevate your life to a higher level of living and consciousness. You are stating that you are ready to become your own source of worthiness and that you will choose your life's intentions and actions consciously, allowing the inner compasses of your deepest being to point you in the direction of True North.

Moving into Your Equilibrium: Week 3 Review

How does it feel to be three-quarters of the way through the program? Good job! You have completed the exercises in the chapters for Week 3 of the Discover True North program:

> ➤ Live Your Fullest Multisensory Life

> ➤ The Four Declarations of Your Authentic Power

Now, take the time to revisit both chapters' lessons and exercises and use the following four steps to reflect on what you learned this week. Allow these four steps to help move you toward your equilibrium for higher learning and understanding.

STEP 1: *Stop and Breathe*

As you begin, clear your mind and reflect on the key points of Week 3 and what you've learned. As before, take a few deep breaths and slowly release them. Relax and consider how the lessons you have gleaned from these chapters might enhance or enlighten your life. Jot down why you feel more aware. Fully appreciate the new or higher perspectives that you may have gained from this week's lessons, and focus on living your most authentic, multisensory life.

STEP 2: *Be Conscious and Think*

How has what you have learned this week served to raise your consciousness about the importance of authentic power? How will you benefit from your multisensory awareness? List some of the ways in which you will activate your awareness levels. Write down what you know to be most important at this time and place in your life. How do you plan to maintain your focus and your attention to the details?

STEP 3: *Choose and Commit*

What life choices will you make and commit to carrying through after completing this week's lessons? In what ways do you anticipate that your choices will move you to a newer, stronger inner wisdom? What moments from this week's lessons represent your deepest truths, ethics, intentions, and beliefs?

STEP 4: *Act and Then Move toward Something*

How do you plan to put into action some of the things you have learned this week? List specific steps that you will take that will move you closer to your True North. What will you need to review and work on for ongoing improvement and personal development? In what time frame will you accomplish this?

Now that you have completed these four steps, you are ready to move on to Week 4, "Romancing Your Potential—Becoming an Upgradable Person."

WEEK
4

Romancing Your Potential—
Becoming an Upgradable Person

9

Cornerstones of Human Potential: Focus, Service, and Gratitude

Higher Purpose Statement

Always strive to be a first-rate version of yourself, knowing that your best, even if it is considered average by others, is good enough if it serves your authentic self. Shed old attitudes about what's in vogue that you may be holding on to and replace them with things that work in your real life. Get focused and stay focused. Serve others and demonstrate your gratitude if you want to be an upgradable person.

How to Romance Your Potential and Upgrade Yourself in the Process

We envy people who are passionate about their work, their love interests, their hobbies, their travels, their creativity, and everything else. We envy them because we, too, want to experience that level of passion and excitement in our lives. Okay, I know what you're thinking: Envy isn't perhaps the most admirable human quality. However, it is certainly a trait that helps to identify and point us toward something that we'd like to have in our lives.

When you romance something or someone, you are saying, "I want to attract this to me and make it part of my life." Your higher potential is something that you must romance if you want to upgrade yourself both personally and professionally. Here, *upgrade* means sharpening your skills, exploring your untapped talents, broadening your horizons, expanding your learning, and putting your greatest capabilities to the test. By romancing your potential, you rediscover yourself and how you perceive things, or, in the words of author Sarah Ban Breathnach, "The lover sees the old anew." Do you see yourself anew?

In her book *Romancing the Ordinary*, Ban Breathnach explains that one of the reasons women crave romance is that it allows them to rediscover themselves and life through someone else's senses. In other words, we stop seeing ourselves and what we have to offer in the same old way. When you romance your potential, you begin appreciating what I call the *average excellence* of life. When we romance our potential, we start to better appreciate who we are and the extraordinary possibilities that lie within each of us. Here's an analogy that I like to use in my seminars.

Let Your Average Excellence Shine!

Astronomers like to point out that our sun is really no big deal—it's just an average star among billions of stars. They are also quick to point out that there are many stars that are hundreds of times larger and more powerful than our sun. Personally, I think this approach compromises and minimizes just how phenomenal our earth's sun is—and that we compromise and minimize how phenomenal each of us can be in the same way. As a result, we stop short of romancing our highest potential, or we cease trying to attract to ourselves greater opportunities and life experiences that would make us upgradable, smarter, and happier people. We keep comparing ourselves to other people's standards of excellence, thereby failing to recognize our own magnificence and to accept that who we are and what we are is good enough in and of itself.

Just like the earth's sun, each of us has the ability to shine brightly among the supernovas of the galaxy in which we live, but in his or her own way, shape, and form. The fact is that our sun is way above average, because it's one of a small minority of stars that can support life as we know it on earth. That's what makes our sun special, not just average. And although the sun may be considered average by many astronomers, it's our sun's *average excellence* that sets it apart from the rest—just as your *average excellence* sets you apart from all the other people on this planet. Romancing the *average excellence* within you is what will ultimately upgrade you as a person. Don't worry about others whom you deem smarter, more attractive, or more charismatic. As I said in the higher purpose statement at the beginning of this chapter, it's time for you to shed the old attitudes about what's in vogue that you may be holding on to and replace them with things that work in your real life.

Consider this: The giant-size stars in our universe are not even around long enough for their planetary systems to settle down and become hospitable, and the tiny stars are so inept that they can provide only a small orbital zone in which water could occur as a liquid—a requisite for earth-like living. And there isn't a planet in one of the two-star systems that would have much chance of evolving life because the conditions are too erratic.

The earth's sun, however, is perfect just the way it is for the development of life—just as you are the perfect person to develop the greater potential within you.

This whole subject is so rich with insights that I hope you will ferret out many of your own. My favorite is this: The most valuable qualities that you possess may not be the most apparent ones—whether that be size, appearance, longevity, or ability to shine among the most brilliant supernovas in the sky. Smaller stars, like the earth's sun, are among the oldest visible bodies in our universe. They burn so slowly they are often the last stars to flicker out, whereas much bigger stars explode before they reach the age that our sun has reached. You know people like this too— they're called "flash in the pans."

My hope is that this chapter will awaken you to the importance of taking the time to romance your potential so that you may become an upgradable person—a person who is always aware of the importance of his or her *average excellence* and unlimited possibilities.

There are three critical cornerstones that contribute greatly to the development of human potential: focus, service, and gratitude. When they are in place, these cornerstones become powerful foundations for upgrading our lives and enhancing our highest potential.

Figure 9-1 shows that focus is one of the cornerstones upon which the ongoing development of our higher potential rests. Another cornerstone is serving humanity—being generous with our time, money, and love, and always giving the best of ourselves. Along with this comes acknowledging and demonstrating our gratitude for all that we have become and all that we possess up to this point.

The Importance of Focus

I have worked with thousands of people in my workshops and seminars over the years, and although my observations may be far from a scientific study, I can assure you that the people whom I've met who demonstrate the ability to pay close attention to their highest potential are the people who discover their True North and stay focused on their North Star in every project they undertake.

It has been my experience that when you master the ability to stay clearly focused on something until its completion, every decision you encounter and

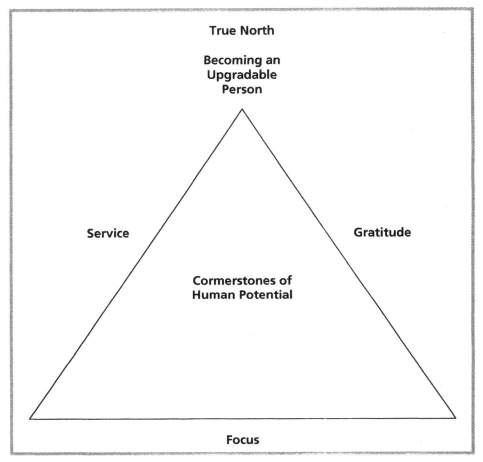

Figure 9-1. True North

every new direction upon which you embark takes on a distinctive path, or map, for getting there.

NAVIGATION TOOL: *Use This Question to Weigh Your Choices*

Focusing on achieving your highest potential requires that you act on your inner truth every moment of your life. It doesn't matter whether you are taking action on behalf of your career, your romantic life, your hobbies, your marriage, or your overall health, or even just choosing the movie you want to see or deciding whether or not to attend someone's dinner party—it all comes down to one critical and navigational question: Does the choice you are about to make serve your greater potential and higher good? If you use this question as the criterion by which you focus your energies and move forward on life's choices, both large and small, you will find yourself getting more clearly focused and becoming better able to reach your greater potential and achieve your most passionate dreams.

LIFE COMPASS: *What Stops You from Focusing?*

What life choices do you make that prevent you from focusing on your greater potential and higher good?

_____

_____

_____

If you were to start making new life choices that focused on your higher potential and greater good, how different do you think your life would be? How, specifically, would it improve? What things would you accomplish that you've always wanted to do but haven't had the focus to complete (write a book, change careers, build a boat, speak French, play the piano, and so on)?

_____

_____

_____

Make a list here of all the things you would like to pursue that would upgrade you as a person and fulfill your higher potential. For each item you list, ask yourself, "Does the choice I am making about this situation really serve my higher potential and greater good in life?" If the answer is no, remove it from your list. If the answer is yes, set in motion a plan of action to focus on and complete the project. Next, assign a date by which you will do this and a separate date for its targeted completion.

_____

_____

_____

Beware of the Distracters: Avoiding the Crazy Things and People That Distract You

Julia Cameron and Mark Bryan, cofounders of the Artist's Way workshops and co-authors of *The Artist's Way at Work* (with Catherine Allen), refer to the people with whom some of us form destructive and distracting alliances as the "Crazymakers." These are people who are known for stirring things up and distracting you from your real focus and higher purpose. Throughout the years, in my own workshops, I have heard similar references, such as "Chaosmakers" or "Crazycreators." However, I still like Cameron and Bryan's term best because these people actually "create" crazy lifestyle situations, crazy relationships, crazy behaviors, crazy classrooms, and crazy, unpredictable, and unnecessary drama. If you are to discover True North and focus on your highest potential, I believe, as Cameron and Bryan do, that you have to avoid these distracters in life. If you don't, they will suck the energy and focus right out of you and distract you to the point where your Inner Guidance System stops functioning and all of your internal compass needles go whacko!

LIFE COMPASS: HOW TO IDENTIFY CRAZY, CHAOTIC DISTRACTERS

There are some fast ways to identify the folks who may well be the greatest distraction from keeping your focus sharp. They...

- ➤ Make you crazy too.

- ➤ Drain your energy with their never-ending dramas.

- ➤ Rarely finish a project and always have an excuse why they can't get it done.

- ➤ Think that everything in their world is an emergency and must be dealt with right now, no matter what you are involved in doing.

- ➤ Never seem truly happy when things aren't out of control.

- ➤ Focus on gloom and doom.

➤ Ask for advice, but never take it.

➤ Have you walking on eggshells so as not to set them off on another drama.

➤ Can embarrass you because of their impatience and rudeness.

➤ Can be husbands, wives, mothers, fathers, sisters, brothers, best friends, neighbors, or anyone else who has access to your life.

Do you have someone in your life who's keeping you from staying focused on what's really important? If the answer is yes, then complete the rest of this exercise.

➤ Name the distracters in your life.

➤ Describe what it is about their behavior that distracts you and keeps you from focusing on developing your higher potential.

Next, learn to set boundaries. These people do not respect other people's goals and greater purpose. They are too caught up in their own out-of-focus world to worry about such things. It's important that you set clear and distinct boundaries with these people. Learn to say no when you have to.

What kind of boundaries can you set with such a person? Be specific and stick to what you say.

Here's an example: "Look Liz, every morning between 8 A.M. and noon, I devote my time to research and writing on my book. Do not call me during these hours or show up at my house unannounced. It is important that I have complete focus and attention on what I am doing during this time each day. If you insist on calling anyway or show up without notice, I will not be able to talk to you or see you. Any time after noon, feel free to call me or to stop by. I will be available then to spend time with you and enjoy your company."

If you can't seem to set clear boundaries with these people, then perhaps you have to ask yourself, as one seminar attendee in my class did, if you like being part of their drama. If you're not avoiding these situations and people, ask yourself, "What am I getting out of this?" or "Why am I choosing to let this person distract me from my focus and from achieving my highest potential?"

Think back to Week 1 in the program, "Do Less of What Lessens You. Do More of What Magnifies Your Soul, Your Gifts, and Your Higher Purpose." This is exactly what I'm talking about here. When you focus, you are magnifying your greater self. When you lose focus, you lessen yourself.

Serving Others Gives Us the Power of Greatness

"Learn to see in another's calamity the ills which you should avoid."—PUBLILIUS SYRUS, AUTHOR (~100 B.C.)

One of my favorite quotes is from Dr. Martin Luther King, Jr. He said, "Everyone has the power for greatness, not for fame but greatness, because greatness is determined by service." If you are going to develop your highest potential, then you must commit yourself to serving others in whatever capacity you are capable of.

The Law of Giving

Serving others is what Deepak Chopra calls the Law of Giving. In his book *The Seven Spiritual Laws of Success*, Chopra discusses the three components of the Law of Dharma. The first is that we are here to discover our true and higher self. The

"When you learn, teach. When you get, give."
—MAYA ANGELOU

second is that we are here to express our unique talents and that every human being has his or her own unique talent to offer. The third component of the Law of Dharma is "service to humanity."

Chopra suggests that each of us ask her- or himself these questions: "How can I help?" and "How can I help those that I come into contact with?" His powerful philosophy encourages each of us to remember that when you combine the ability to express your unique talent with service to humanity, and couple this with your pure potentiality and spirituality, you will have unlimited access to abundance.

NAVIGATIONAL TOOL: *The Two A's*

In my workshops I talk about two very important navigational tools called the two A's—attention and appreciation. We automatically serve others when we offer them our undivided attention or time and genuine appreciation. It never ceases to amaze me how just a few kind words or a gesture of thoughtfulness can make a person's day. It takes so little to boost someone's mood or confidence, yet the effects are contagious and long-lasting.

When you serve others and give to others, everyone you touch feels more abundant, and that abundance will be passed on to others.

LIFE COMPASS: *The Law of Physics*

I am confident that whatever you pass on to others, good or bad, comes back to you. No, this is not a course I developed. It's a law of physics. Life is an energy exchange. We give and we receive. When you give what it is you want or need in your own life, you will receive those same things in abundance. I believe in this universal law, also known as cause and effect, and I also believe that this law applies to each one of us, not just physically, but emotionally and spiritually as well.

Here's something to think about: You attract to you what you give away. Respond to the following statements in this Life Compass.

The Energy Exchange—Attracting What You Give

Respond to the following:

What do I desire to have more of in my life? Make a list here. Your list may include things such as laughter, patience, compassion, love, generosity, meaningful relationships, and so on.

_____

_____

_____

Keep in mind what I said earlier: You attract what you give to others. So, if you say that you are in need of more understanding and compassion from others, ask yourself, "How can I be more understanding and tolerant of those around me? How can I show more of my compassion to those who need it most?" In other words, be other-centered, not self-centered. You wouldn't ask yourself, "What can I do to get people to show me their compassion?" or "What can I do to get other people to understand my needs and wants?"

Now list some of the ways in which you can start serving others and giving of yourself. For example, if you are in need of friends, list some of the ways you can be a friend to others.

_____

_____

_____

Serving Others Helps Us Achieve Our Highest Potential

Here are some of the ways you can commit to serving others with greater generosity:

1. Bring your special brand of gifts to all those whom you encounter. I am not speaking of gifts that you buy in a store. I am speaking of gifts such as a compliment, a helping hand, a prayer, your patience, a sympathetic ear, empathy, or your undivided attention.

2. Be committed to circulating feelings of appreciation, compassion, affection, caring, and love wherever you go.

3. Select your own favorite charity and make monthly donations.

4. Volunteer.

5. Be spontaneous with your generosity. If someone is cold and is wearing an old coat, buy that person a new and better one, or give her or him yours.

6. Give with pure intention, not with motive. If you expect to be recognized for your generosity, you defeat the purpose. Try giving something anonymously.

> "Ambition without contribution is of no significance."—KEVIN KLINE AS MR. HUNDERT IN THE MOVIE *THE EMPEROR'S CLUB*

The main thing to remember about serving humanity is to serve others with a clear and purposeful intention. This means wanting someone else to receive the pleasure of your giving and service just for the joy of it.

What Goes Around, Comes Around

Don't look at the world as a piece of pie—if I give you a slice, there will be one less slice left for me. The more you give, the more there will be for you to give. Whatever you give away, you will eventually get back in one form or another. And by the same token, whatever you withhold will be withheld from you.

You will develop the courage, self-confidence, and character to fulfill your highest potential when you choose to serve others.

Longitude, Altitude, and Gratitude

We have come to the third cornerstone of developing your greater potential: gratitude.

During this program, you've traveled the longitude of east and west to get to this point in Week 4. You've been required to soar at a higher altitude in order to gain a clearer perspective on where you're going and what you want to achieve when you get there. Now it all comes down to gratitude—a pivotal cornerstone for realizing your higher calling and greatest gifts.

If you do not acknowledge your gratitude, you cannot move up to a higher level of purpose and a higher level of appreciation for all that you have at this moment in time.

My friend Marci, who is the famous artist and creator of the inspirational Children of the Inner Light dolls, greeting cards, and more, reminds me that "gratitude is a gift I can choose each day." She also reminded me recently in a telephone conversation that by living in a space of gratitude and acceptance, we can find life's deepest purpose in relationships. But do we demonstrate our gratitude and thankfulness for those relationships? "It is our connections with our parents, our children, our spouses, our siblings, and our friends that provide us with lasting joy," says Marci. I happen to agree with her. We take so much for granted, always dwelling on what we wish we had rather than focusing on being grateful for all that we've got, whether that be in the form of relationships, possessions, talent, opportunity, or deep-down, unconditional faith that whatever life throws at you, you'll get through it.

Even your memories are something to be extremely grateful for. Take a moment here to reflect on four of your life's memories for which you are thankful. Write them down, and if they involve friends or family, call those people now and tell them how you are feeling and what their part in your memories means to you.

NAVIGATIONAL TOOL: *Just Say "Thank You"*

I have learned over the years that one of the strongest, most reliable navigational tools that I can count on when I feel lost or when I have veered from my path toward True North boils down to two words: Thank you! If saying "thank you" doesn't get you back on course in a hurry, nothing will.

Maybe you're saying to yourself, what is she talking about? What am I supposed to be saying "thank you" for? And to whom am I saying it? The answer is, you're saying "thank you" to a higher power for everything you do have, not focusing on what you don't have. Even in the face of adversity, you can find seeds of hope, joy, and prosperity.

To help you along, here are some of the things for which I have said "thank you," in the past few years.

Some days I give thanks for simple things, like, "Thank you for reminding me how much I love to watch the sun set," or, "Thank you for bringing my cat home after 2 days and nights in the cold and rain." Maybe I'm just thankful that I didn't over-cook the linguine for a small but important dinner party that I was hosting.

Other times, I give thanks for bigger things, like my plane landing safely in a bad storm. I've given thanks many times over the years for the special gift of being with those I loved most when they died, like my mother, a dear friend, and my father-in-law. I recall my enormous gratitude and thanks for the gifted surgeons who once operated on my daughter.

I find that when I record my gratitude and write it down, each moment of thankfulness and appreciation takes on more meaning for me personally.

So that is what I am going to recommend that you do now in the following Life Compass. Maybe you already have what is often called a "gratitude journal." But if you don't, now is a good time to start one, before you complete this program. I guarantee that it will transform your life and upgrade you in the process.

> **"Gratitude unlocks the fullness of life. It turns what we have into enough, and more. It turns denial into acceptance, chaos to order, confusion to clarity. It can turn a meal into a feast, a house into a home, a stranger into a friend. Gratitude makes sense of our past, brings peace for today, and creates a vision for tomorrow."**
> —MELODY BEATTIE, AUTHOR OF *JOURNEY TO THE HEART: DAILY MEDITATIONS ON THE PATH TO FREEING YOUR SOUL*

LIFE COMPASS: *Inner Exploration—Record Your Thankfulness*

Writing down your innermost thoughts of appreciation in a journal can be a valuable tool for inner exploration as you move toward True North. Journaling your gratitude can greatly enhance the quality of your life and, in turn, your potential. When you examine your gratitude in words, it changes who you are and what you know to be important in life. Journaling your thankfulness becomes a daily reminder of the abundance you have in your life, and that abundance often becomes the most motivating and inspiring part of your day.

First, find a quiet spot where you can record your feelings of thankfulness.

Then ask yourself: What things in my life do I have to be grateful for that I may be overlooking or taking for granted?

What to Do When Gratitude Doesn't Come Easily

Sure, it's easy to be grateful when your life is in good order, the bills are paid, your family's health is good, and there's money in the bank.

But what if that's not the case? What if you're in misery and pain? What are you supposed to do? How are you supposed to record your thankfulness when you have just been laid off from your job, lost a friend in a car accident, or suffered a broken heart when you lost the love of your life to another? Believe it or not, sometimes it is when we are in the greatest pain that we can be the most thankful, because our hardship somehow delivers lessons that refine and build our character and our soul.

Gratitude is not measured by *how* you feel during the worst of times; rather, it involves acknowledging that something good still exists for you. I'll share with you this personal example.

A very close friend of mine was in devastating pain and mourning after the senseless and random murder of her 24-year-old son. In the depths of her greatest sorrow, however, she somehow found something to be grateful for and hold on to.

She told me that on that particular day, while she was attending a support-group meeting for parents of murdered children, she listened to the unimaginable ways in which some parents had lost their children to violent crimes. Afterward, she expressed to me that if her son had to be taken in such a violent way, she was somehow grateful that he had been shot in the head suddenly and had never known what happened to him. From the depths of her soul, she managed to find thankfulness in knowing that her son had died immediately and without prolonged suffering. I never forgot her courageous words. As a mother myself, I couldn't imagine finding any good in such a horrific situation. I learned a great deal about the sanctity of gratitude from my friend that day.

> **"Gratitude is the most exquisite form of courtesy."**
> **—JACQUES MARITAIN, FRENCH PHILOSOPHER AND POLITICAL THINKER**

Navigational Tools for Expressing Gratitude

One of the most well-known ways in which we've learned about recording our thanks is from Sarah Ban Breathnach and her famous journaling book, *The Simple Abundance Gratitude Journal.* Several of her journals are available, including a leather-bound edition. Other gratitude journals that you can find in bookstores or order online include *Attitudes of Gratitude Journal,* by M. J. Ryan; *Soul Catcher,* by Kathy and Amy Eldon; and *Daily Riches: A Journal of Gratitude and Awareness,* by Jane Bluestein, Judy Lawrence, and S. J. Sanchez. You can also go to any stationery store or bookstore and select the prettiest or sturdiest blank book you can find to use as your journal. Some people use blank pages in prayer books or traditional diaries, complete with ribbon and gold clasp.

The point is this: Learn to be grateful, no matter what you have or what has happened in your life.

We're All in This Together

What we do solely for ourselves dies with us. What we do for ourselves so that we may reach our higher potential and greater good while serving others and demonstrating our gratitude will echo throughout the ages.

As human beings, we are designed to reach for the best within ourselves. We are meant to serve and be served. Take a moment to reflect on three things that you would not change in your life, then record them in your journal. Speak them aloud and tell those you love the things for which you are most appreciative.

In the words of Rabbi Abraham Heschel, "Just to be is a blessing. Just to live is holy." Live your most reverent life, knowing that no one is smarter than all of us combined.

10

Simplicity and the Einstein Approach to Bringing Forth Your Own Genius

Higher Purpose Statement

Simplifying life is a process. This process may even be part of our genetic make-up—the desire to live more fully and with greater joy and purpose may be an inner programming to be happy and to contribute the best of ourselves while we are on this planet. Living a more simple life does not mean making do with less. It means learning to appreciate the important things in life a little bit more. Simplicity requires "mindful living," a sort of living-on-purpose approach to enhancing the quality of our lives. Taking a simple approach to things enables us to find solutions faster and to approach the most complex problems by reducing them to their simplest terms, a characteristic that Albert Einstein was famous for practicing. And just like Einstein, when we strive for simplicity, we bring forth our own genius.

Deprivation Is Not Simplicity, nor Is It Recommended

If you think that simplifying your life requires giving up food, housing, clothing, and medical treatment, you're wrong; it doesn't. In fact, in my opinion, that's not simplicity, that's voluntary impoverishment!

We've all read magazine articles about the classic yuppie couple with the six-figure income who become fed up with their fast-track careers, 4-hours-a-day commute time, and pitiful family life. So what do they do? They seek a life of greater simplicity by giving away all their worldly possessions and moving out to the boonies, a hundred miles from nowhere, to live a more "authentic" life—a life without running water, electricity, plumbing, or any other modern conveniences. Excuse me, Swiss Family Robinson, but I'll take the less-simple life—and I'll keep my dishwasher, my microwave, my washing machine, and my dryer, thank you!

How Real People Approach Simplicity

You'll be glad to know that only a very small percentage of people choose such a drastic change in lifestyle in their quest for simplicity. Studies show that people who simplify successfully continue to live conventional lives. They go on working for a living, taking their kids to day care, and planning summer vacations, just like everyone else. After all, they're real people, like you and me. But here's what they do differently: They find a way to trade in their more stressful living habits for "lighter" living habits. That means that they become more mindful of their lifestyles and the effects of those lifestyles on their overall happiness and health. They choose lighter living, as opposed to heavy, drag-you-down, make-you-sick, shorten-your-life-significantly living. So what exactly is lighter living all about—what I refer to in my workshops for fun as "simplicity lite"?

Simplicity Lite

Just like the beer in the ad, "simplicity lite" is less filling and more satisfying. Why do we always associate getting back to a simpler, more fulfilling life with rejecting all of our material possessions and creature comforts? In fact, in most cases, giving up some of these things would cause greater stress and more complicated living.

There is only one requirement for adopting the "simplicity lite" way of living, and that is that you begin, one step at a time, to unburden yourself of life's distractions and its overwhelming, sometimes energy-sucking activities and relationships—or anything else that interferes with your achieving and living a better-quality life. Don't expect to be able to do it all overnight. Getting to simplicity is a process. But you can start the process right here, right now.

NAVIGATION TOOL: *This Way to Living Lite*

I want you to get into the mindset of "unburdening" your life. Using the following Life Compass, I would like you to begin by listing some of the things that you have control of in your life and that you can change right away. (If you start with things that you can easily control, you will see immediate results, and that will build your confidence for further unburdening down the road.) These are things that have a significant impact on the complexity of the way you are living and that can either inhibit or enhance the level of joy and meaning in your life. In addition, I would like you to select the specific action steps that you will take to make this unburdening process a reality. This exercise will guide you in examining each area of your life, starting with your personal happiness, then going on to your work situation, your social life, your financial endeavors, your physical and emotional health, and your spiritual well-being.

The idea is to look closely at each part of your life and to begin lifting one or two burdens from each area right away. By doing this, you will almost immediately feel a sense of release.

For example, in one of my workshops, I had a woman who decided right then and there to have the Sunday family dinners at her house every other Sunday, instead of every Sunday. She later told me that having that break every other week made her life much easier and that she was actually better able to enjoy her family because she wasn't so exhausted. What action did she put into play to make this a reality? She called two of her cousins and asked them to help cover every other Sunday dinner. They agreed, and Janet's life became simpler and less stressful as a result.

In the same workshop, a young widowed father of two girls decided to go to his supervisor and ask if he could work from home just 1 day a week. He wanted to do this so that he could be with his girls in the morning, help them get ready for school, have breakfast with them, and then drive them to school. With this new arrangement, he would also be able to pick them up after school, make them a snack, and help them with their homework. Mark felt that up to now he had been missing out on being part of his daughters' early childhood morning and afternoon routines. He felt that by being able to work from home 1 day a week, he would be experiencing an important part of his daughters' lives that he was now missing. His supervisor agreed to the arrangement, and Mark is now enjoying the little things he was missing before with his kids—the simple things.

LIFE COMPASS: *Navigating a Course to Simplicity*

Unburdening Your Life One Piece at a Time

In your *day-to-day personal life*, what can you do right now to simplify your life and appreciate the little things—things that make life more enjoyable for you and those you love?

_____

_____

What action steps will be required in order to make this a reality?

_____

_____

In your *work life*, what can you do to simplify things on the job and make the time you spend doing your work more enjoyable?

_____

_____

What action steps will be required in order to make this a reality?

_____

_____

In your *social life*, what can you do to simplify your commitments and make your social activities more enjoyable?

_____

_____

What action steps will be required in order to make this a reality?

_____

_____

In your *financial endeavors*, what can you do to reduce your expenses and establish financial tranquility in your life?

_____

_____

What action steps will be required in order to make this a reality?

_____

_____

For the sake of your *physical and emotional well-being*, what simple steps can you take that will boost your energy and make you stronger, both inside and out?

_____

_____

What action steps will be required in order to make this a reality?

_____

_____

In your *spiritual life*, what can you do to co-create a simpler and more gratifying lifestyle? What would make your life more meaningful and soulful? What simple spiritual practices, like prayer or meditation, will provide you with greater inner peace and joy?

_____

_____

What action steps will be required in order to make this a reality?

_____

_____

Life Compass Review

Take a look at all your responses. How will embracing a life of greater simplicity and joy, purpose and balance, help you to better navigate your journey to True North? How do you see these things as being linked? By taking these action steps to eliminate stresses and slowly unburden your life, you will be on your way to greater happiness and peace of mind.

"A sound mind in a sound body, is a short but full description of a happy state in this world."—JOHN LOCKE, ENGLISH PHILOSOPHER

Jonathan's Story

Back when I was a senior partner in the third-largest law firm in Massachusetts, I can honestly say that I was out of whack. At least, that's my best definition of myself back then. If success, productivity, and material gain are addictive, then I was an addict. I was the classic type-A personality, getting the most out of every day—talking on the phone while driving, helping my sons with homework while cooking dinner and watching the six o'clock news. Instead of walking to meetings, I ran. Instead of planning quiet time for myself, I'd squeeze in errands and fill my weekends with more work.

I didn't just wake up one morning and decide to seek a more meaningful and fulfilling life. It took me about 20 years to wake up, but the point is, I did. You could say that I pushed myself to the limits, but I think I pushed myself beyond the limits.

I knew I'd reached the breaking point of my success when my inner truth, my authentic self, my soul, turned me inside out and forced me to look at what was really important. Oh, yeah, did I mention the mild heart attack? Actually that was my wake-up call. I was only 39, and I had already suffered my first heart attack. That's when the bells rang and the lights flashed. This life of mine made no sense whatsoever. It was time to downshift this race car I called a body.

Here are some of the things I did when I downshifted my life to one of greater simplicity and happiness. It's still amazing to me that simplifying just a few behaviors would have such a large impact on my life and how I felt. I no longer just practice law; I practice simplicity wherever and whenever I can. Here are a few things that have worked for me:

➤ I build in buffer time between appointments. Instead of having meetings back to back, I purposely build in at least 45 minutes between appointments, and an hour when that's possible. It is amazing how that small amount of extra time to myself gives me the space I need in order to decompress and gather my thoughts before the next meeting. I think I'm a better lawyer for it, and clients tell me that I seem less frantic these days.

➤ I take the phone off the hook for at least 2 hours when I get home. This may sound ridiculous, but it works for me. There are no interruptions, and I can concentrate on talking with my sons. The phone doesn't ring off the hook while we are having dinner, and as a result we all have a more enjoyable meal together.

➤ I limit my social commitments to two a month. Previously, I was actually attending as many as eight social engagements a month, most of which I couldn't have cared less about. Now I'm more particular about where and with whom I spend my discretionary time.

➤ I downsized many of the material possessions, or, in my case, trappings, of my life. I sold two of my four cars. Who needs four cars? I had a garage sale and got rid of a lot of stuff I didn't need, stuff that not only cluttered my closets, but also cluttered my mind. I feel freer for having done so, and I swear I can think more clearly now. It's amazing how much lighter we feel when we purge ourselves of unnecessary things.

➤ I got a dog. I don't know what it is, but somehow having a dog makes me feel more grounded and connected to nature and animals. It's a feeling that somehow I know that we are all connected in some way.

I'm no expert on simplicity. I know that I still have a long way to go when it comes to slowing down and smelling the roses, as they say. But I've come a long way, and I'm glad to say that taking small steps, one at a time, rather than trying to overhaul my entire life overnight, has allowed me to ease into this new simple-living lifestyle. And it's a lifestyle that I plan on living for a long, long time.

"To prolong life, worry less."
—CHINESE PROVERB

Simplicity Is in the Eye of the Beholder

Studies on simple living show that there are no hard and fast rules for living the simple life, and that living more simply means different things to different people. For example, a couple who lives in a 3000-square-foot home, complete with expensive-to-maintain furnishings, landscaping, and property, might consider downsizing to a luxury two-bedroom condo to be a simple, less stressful, better way to live.

Another couple may be quite comfortable with the materially rich life that they've earned, but may feel the need to simplify in a different way—perhaps through connecting to and exploring their religious or spiritual interests at a deeper level. For this couple, living more simply might involve spending less time at work and making a greater time commitment to their community, church, or synagogue. Or it might mean volunteering to work with Habitat for Humanity or Junior Achievement. At some point, this couple might even want to put their life on hold, take a sabbatical, and join the Peace Corps for 2 years. Doing so wouldn't require that they relinquish all their worldly possessions; they would just have to carve out a chunk of time that would enable them to gain the inner fulfillment they are seeking and then incorporate those experiences into their daily lives upon their return.

Then there are people who view a simpler lifestyle as meaning a way to connect with Mother Earth. One couple I know moved to a farm in Wisconsin so that they could live off the land. They love it there, but that doesn't mean that they don't use electricity and all the other modern conveniences that make life's chores more manageable. Another friend of mine sees simple living as her small Greenwich Village studio apartment, in the heart of New York City, with just a few pieces of thrift-store furniture. My friend contends that a humble lifestyle is the trade-off for her being able to afford to live in the city she loves most.

For many people, yearning for simplicity leads to making simple changes—changes that can enhance life almost immediately. These things may include job sharing, developing stronger intimacy with family and friends, or celebrating holidays in a less stressful fashion by putting limits on gift giving and spending, or they may involve taking what could have been a devastating situation and turning it into something adventurous and meaningful. Here's a personal story that I'd like to share with you.

Losing Your Job Can Be *Simply* Wonderful!

A few years back, when the high-tech industry in California's Silicon Valley took a dive, my daughter Autumn was working there as a trainer for an international software company. With two degrees from Notre Dame University, a super apartment in the upscale San Francisco neighborhood Russian Hill, a new SUV, a great salary, and perks to match, life for my daughter was good—and yet it was filled with all the daily stresses that living and working in the big city can bring. But her life was about to get a whole lot simpler.

It was a Friday morning when the phone rang, and it was Autumn. She sounded upbeat as always: "Hi, mom!" Then came the next sentence: "I just lost my job." At first I thought I'd heard wrong because she sounded so happy, not at all like someone who'd just been laid off.

My first words were, "Are you all right, honey?" "I'm great!" came the reply, without hesitation. "I'm driving over to my travel agent's office now to pick up the 'round-the-world' ticket I just bought with my severance pay." I couldn't believe my ears. Then came words of wisdom from my 26-year-old daughter that I'll never forget.

"Mom, life's too short and I'm too young for this rat race. I want to see the world. I want to simplify my life. I'm going to sell my clothes, sell my car, give up my place overlooking San Francisco Bay, and backpack around the world."

To make a long story short, that's exactly what Autumn did, and my husband, David, and I were thrilled for her—even though I worried nonstop the entire 9 months she was gone. We have always encouraged our kids to follow their dreams and just go for it. This wasn't the time to renege on our parental philosophies.

What had been a devastating experience for some of her coworkers became a life-changing adventure for my daughter—an adventure in which learning to simplify and getting along just fine with less was the ultimate destination.

Autumn quickly learned that a backpack, a few Gap T-shirts, cargo pants, Tevas, and a few personal necessities were enough to enable her to live happily for a long period of time. She also learned that finding real happiness in life isn't about the prestigious job, the new car, the terrific apartment, or having great clothes—not that it's not okay to have those things. Of course it is. But having them isn't everything, and if you can still be happy without all of life's material possessions, then when you do have them, you can appreciate them that much more.

It didn't take long for Autumn to realize that she had more worldly possessions in that backpack of hers than most of the people in the world have—especially those that she encountered and lived among in the most isolated regions of China and Vietnam, or in the most remote jungles of northern Thailand—where she hiked for hours and then, with a guide, rode an elephant to find the closest tribe. She was carrying her life on her back, and that was all she needed, because she was already blessed with a wealth of inner peace, serenity, self-confidence, compassion, common sense, and intelligence—all reliable life compasses.

My daughter's journey to discovering greater happiness by living a simpler and more gratifying life has been a source of great inspiration for me. I marvel at

Autumn's courageous and uncompromising determination to follow her dreams. Most recently those dreams have taken her across the Pacific Ocean to Hawaii, where she is working with some of the world's finest dolphin behaviorists and trainers conducting dolphin encounters for children and adults, in an effort to create greater public awareness of the vital importance of marine life to our planet. And so my daughter's journey toward True North continues, but it continues with fewer of life's trappings and a greater appreciation of life's little treasures.

Bringing Forth Your Own Genius

We all have models that we turn to for guidance when we are seeking calm and simpler things in our life. For some it's been Gandhi, His Holiness the Dalai Lama, or Thoreau; in my case, it's always been Albert Einstein.

Einstein wrote a good deal about simplicity. One of his famous quotes that I enjoy is, "Everything should be made as simple as possible, but not simpler." His approach to life, despite his genius, was one of simple understanding. And although he refined his theory of relativity to the simplest equation, $E = Mc^2$, Einstein died a frustrated man because he had not been able to further simplify the theory.

I particularly like to use Einstein's approach to simplicity when I am facilitating a workshop or a class. Like Einstein, I believe that the really intelligent people of the world have the ability to take the complex and make it simple. I have used this approach and the illustration in Figure 10-1 in my teaching methods for years.

Specifically, Einstein listed the levels of intelligence in this order: "Smart, intelligent, brilliant, genius, simple" (see Figure 10-1). There are stories about Einstein's frustration with fellow professors at Princeton University—colleagues who would gather to discuss and contemplate issues of great complexity, sometimes deliberately maintaining their complexity, perhaps in an attempt to fuel their own ego. When this happened, Einstein is said to have walked away in disgust. He had little patience with people who didn't simplify when things could be made easier to understand.

"I notice that you use plain, simple short words, and brief sentences. That is the way to write English. It is the modern way and the best way. Stick to it."
—MARK TWAIN, IN A LETTER TO A YOUNG WRITER

Slow Down

By choosing simplicity in your life, you are choosing to slow down and navigate toward a more rewarding way of living. It is then that simplicity becomes a powerful and inspirational compass.

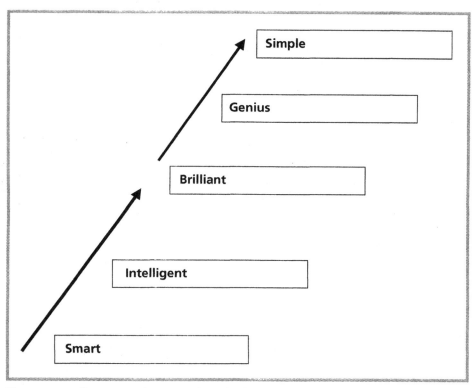

Figure 10-1. Einstein's Theory on Levels of Intelligence

By reducing the complexities of your life and bringing forth your common sense and personal genius, you will become better equipped to contribute to your inner growth and personal development. So spend some time thinking about the things you can do to make your life easier and more enjoyable. Simplifying can help you to create the inner peace you are seeking and the stability you require in order to continue your journey toward your True North.

Moving into Your Equilibrium: Week 4 Review

You have completed the exercises in the chapters for Week 4 of the Discover True North program:

- ➤ Cornerstones of Human Potential: Focus, Service, and Gratitude
- ➤ Simplicity and the Einstein Approach to Bringing Forth Your Own Genius

Now take the time to revisit both chapters' lessons and exercises and use the following four steps to reflect on what you learned this week. Allow these four steps to help move you toward your equilibrium for higher learning and understanding.

STEP 1: *Stop and Breathe*

As you begin, clear your mind and reflect on the key points of Week 4 and what you've learned. As before, take a few deep breaths and slowly release them. Relax and consider how the lessons you have gleaned from these chapters might enhance or enlighten your life. Jot down ways in which you feel more aware. Fully appreciate the new or higher perspectives that you may have gained from this week's lessons by focusing on the cornerstones of your human potential and the new simplicity that you will bring to your life.

> "Nothing is more simple than greatness; indeed, to be simple is to be great."
> —RALPH WALDO EMERSON

STEP 2: *Be Conscious and Think*

How has what you have learned this week served to raise your consciousness about the importance of simplifying your life and unburdening yourself of stresses? How will you benefit from your greater awareness since completing this week's lessons? Write down what you know to be most important at this time and place in your life. How do you plan to maintain your focus, service to others, and gratitude?

STEP 3: *Choose and Commit*

What life choices will you make and commit to carrying through after completing this week's lessons? How do you anticipate that your choices will move you closer to True North and a life of greater simplicity and peace of mind? What resonates within you?

STEP 4: *Act and Then Move toward Something*

How do you plan to put into action some of the things that you have learned this week? List specific steps that you will take that will move you closer to your True North. What will you need to review and work on for ongoing improvement and personal development? In what time frame will you accomplish this?

Now that you have completed these four steps, you are ready to move on to the conclusion of the Discover True North program. You're almost there!

CONCLUSION

Why You Matter and Why This Program Matters

I believe in you. You matter and this program matters because there is more to each one of us than we could ever imagine. And because of that, we all need tools and resources, like this book, to help us along. We want navigation tools that will guide us, a step at a time, toward our greater potential and toward becoming all that we can be. In the words of writer Robert Fritz, "One of the most important things you can bring into this world is the you that you really want to be."

You Are Greater Than You Think You Are

Dr. Norman Vincent Peale once said, "You are greater than you think you are." I believe that each of us has the ability to do something significant and great—something that can change the world for the better in some way, large or small. In fact, I bet you've already done such things in your lifetime through choices you have made, or people you have reached out to and have touched or influenced. You deserve to know the impact that you make on the world and on others. That is why I wrote this book: so that each reader could come to understand and appreciate the special qualities of his or her own True North—Polaris—the navigational star that shines within each person.

Harnessing the Force That Binds Us

We are all connected to one another by a force far greater than ourselves. You may call this force love, energy, spirit, God, or higher consciousness. The label you place on it doesn't really matter. What matters is that you somehow learn to harness that

> The Chinese have two distinct characters for the word *crisis*. One means "danger," and the other means "opportunity."

force, perhaps using some of the tools and exercises in this book, to grow yourself, expand your mind, and endure the most difficult challenges that life hands you.

Yes, bad things happen to people. We get sick. Someone we love dies. The company we work for collapses. Sometimes we are destructive to ourselves and to others—we eat too much or drink too much, or we hurt the ones we love with harsh words or irresponsible actions. But I believe that, whatever the crises we may face or the dreadful times we may endure throughout our life, within every crisis there is hidden possibility and opportunity that rouses the human spirit to rise above it all and dance again.

You Are the Author of Your Life Story

Congratulations on completing this 4-week program. I hope you will not forget that you are the author of your life story—that no one other than you can dream your dreams or navigate the course of your destiny.

The day you came into this world, an amazing gift was bestowed upon you: the gift of becoming the author of your life story—a story like no one else's in this world. When you choose to take charge and become the author of your life story, you take complete responsibility for your life. Your mantra becomes "No martyrs; no victims." You make a conscious decision to fully accept ownership of and personal accountability for where you will go and how you will get there.

> "Hope begins in the dark, the stubborn hope that if you just show up and try to do the right thing, the dawn will come. You wait and watch and work: you don't give up."—ANNE LAMOTT, *BIRD BY BIRD*

With this pivotal decision comes great power. Every person whom you encounter and every experience that you enter into represents an opportunity for you to be guided by your True North and to become your most authentic and powerful self. The things you've learned up to this point will provide you with what you need to make any necessary changes in your life story. Maybe that means making changes in things that no longer serve your greater purpose and desires, like a struggling and energy-depleting relationship or a long-overdue career move.

No matter where you are in your life at this moment in time, or how lonely and desperate you may be feeling, know that you and you alone own the decision to embrace or not to embrace True North and a path of greater possibility and hope for a better tomorrow. The important thing is always to navigate toward hope.

Navigating toward Hope

I believe that people will persevere and rise above the odds if they believe that there is hope. Let your natural instincts become your inner compass when you are navigating toward hope. We all have instincts of survival within us that we can call upon when we are confronting life's most difficult times. Our instincts take our natural resilience and make it our personal declaration of hope. It is then that hope becomes an ongoing source of revitalization, and even heroism when necessary.

A Real-Life Navigator of Hope

I was first introduced to Dr. Pam Hinds, director of nursing research at St. Jude Children's Research Hospital in Memphis, Tennessee, while I was writing another book, on the subject of building hope and morale in the workplace, post–September 11. It hit me after the interview that this woman had tenets that were critical navigation tools that we can all use and learn from.

Dr. Hinds has been dealing with the survival and hope of her patients, their families, and her staff for more than 18 years. In an environment in which catastrophic childhood illnesses are a daily reality, Dr. Hinds has helped to create an environment for her staff in which hope and belief in a higher purpose for all of us are the orders of the day.

"I point out to people that this work is not about focusing on the intensity of sadness and death that can result from these illnesses. Instead we learn to focus on the moment-to-moment miracles that happen here, at St. Jude, every single day. If you stop focusing on all of the remarkable possibilities, there can be chaos," says Dr. Hinds.

Here are some of the suggestions that Dr. Hinds offers her staff when it comes to sustaining and navigating toward hope in an environment in which fear for what might be and hope for what can be come together on a daily basis.

➤ Never sacrifice human connection for productivity.

➤ Honor every relationship.

➤ Be a real person to those who need you—get involved with their lives.

➤ Focus on what is most meaningful to others and meet those human needs as best you can.

➤ Understand that much can be said with few words.

➤ Have a mission, because when the mission is clear, as it is at St. Jude (to find cures for children with catastrophic illnesses through research and treatment), you will draw the right people to you.

➤ In the midst of extreme intensity and sadness, always point to the many miracles of survival that surround you.

➤ Remember that everything good that you do goes beyond the walls of where you live and work.

➤ Understand that even dying patients have hope and that it is your job to help sustain that hope. For example, a young patient at St. Jude who knows that he or she is going to die may hold high hopes for the happiness of his or her parents, siblings, and friends.

➤ Look to the future, and share your hope and your belief in miracles.

Starting at the End

The Discover True North program really starts as this book comes to an end. I say this to you because this program requires ongoing work and a lifelong commitment to personal growth. The work never stops, and the rewards you will reap as a result won't stop either. However, along the way, you may need some help or additional support in continuing the process. When you need help or support ask for it.

Ask for Help When You Need It, Then Accept It

I hope that those of you for whom this book has proved to be a helpful guide in your pursuit of True North will somehow find a way to continue with the process and share this book with others.

"The area where we are the greatest is the area in which we inspire, encourage, and connect with another human being."—MAYA ANGELOU

My suggestion is this: If, after working through this program, you need additional help or support for your efforts, ask for it. Seek out mentors and coaches, then gratefully accept the help you are offered. Sometimes our greatest challenge in life is not extending help to others, but accepting help when we need it ourselves. Here are a few suggestions for continuing the process that you have started by reading this book and participating in this program.

Continuing What You've Started

One way to continue on your journey to True North is to start a Discover True North Expedition Group. The purpose of starting such a group is to enjoy the exploration process and to get pleasure and support from others who are on similar paths and who share similar interests. This book will serve as a valuable catalyst for thoughtful questions and ongoing meaningful dialogue.

Tips for Starting Your Own Discover True North Expedition Group

If you are interested in putting together a group of people to further the work in this book, here are some suggestions for getting started.

1. Invite Like-Minded People to Join You

For example, enlist people who meet the following criteria: (1) They are deeply interested in exploring the subject matter in this book; (2) you feel comfortable talking openly and honestly with them; (3) they will agree to meet on a regular basis; (4) they are willing to read the book and do the exercises; and (5) they are willing to contribute ideas and honest input—that is, they are comfortable with interactive exercises and meaningful discussion.

2. Facilitating the Group

- ➤ Have at least four participants.

- ➤ Designate a leader or facilitator for each meeting to help the flow of discussion and to introduce new ideas.

- ➤ Select a specific topic or assignment for each meeting ahead of time, and distribute it to all attendees by email.

- ➤ Use the weekly sessions from this book, especially the exercises, to focus your discussions and enable you to grow.

- ➤ Set a schedule for people's initial commitment to the process—for example, twice a month, once a week for 2 months, or once a month for 6 months.

- ➤ Meet for a designated length of time: for example, 1 hour or 2 hours.

➤ Decide when sessions should be held: at breakfast, at lunch, after work, at dinner, on weekends, or at other specified times.

➤ Allow the group to discover what works best in terms of format, pace, and focus.

➤ Discuss ground rules for group members, such as: no one tells someone what she or he *should* do, although suggestions are welcome, or everyone's privacy will be respected and their information kept confidential.

The Most Famous Discovery Group of All

Did you know that many of the self-discovery groups we know of today are actually patterned after a group started by Benjamin Franklin back in 1727? He called it the Junto, and its members met every Friday night in a room over a Philadelphia tavern. Franklin was known to say that the club was the best school of philosophy, morals, and politics. Every meeting opened with a set of questions—some practical, some pious. The Junto went on for 30 years.

For more information on starting your own Discover True North Expedition Group, visit www.annebruce.com and click on the Discover True North link. There you will find a Discover True North Group Study Guide that you can print out and use for facilitating your own ongoing program. In addition, at this link you will be guided to other helpful resources and learning tools that support the 4-week program that you've now concluded. This site also lists ways to bring a Discover True North workshop or keynote presentation to your organization, church, or association. Or you can email me directly for more information at anne@annebruce.com.

Your Soul Map and Your Sacred Agreement

At the beginning of this book, I asked you to make three life-changing commitments—commitments that would place you on a more direct path to getting the most out of this program. To refresh your memory, let's look again at these three commitments. They are:

1. Make your personal growth and self-development a top priority.

2. Use your intellect and your faith in tandem.

3. Focus on the present and start living forward.

What I didn't tell you early in the book was that these three commitments would later become specific directives, and that upon the completion of this program, they would become mile markers on your soul map that would help orient you on your journey toward True North. Whenever you are feeling lost or slightly off track, refer to these three commitments to calibrate the needle on any one of the life compasses we've covered in this book. Then prepare to have your soul map guide you back to your personal, one-of-a-kind, exciting, uncharted path, inspiring you to venture into unknown realms of personal discovery. Each commitment will call to you to become a visionary for your own life—to see beyond the ordinary and pursue the quest to *know thyself.*

Now that you've almost finished this book, I'm going to ask you to make a Sacred Agreement with yourself to keep these important commitments strong—a promise to develop each commitment to a higher level of personal insight and self-discovery on an ongoing basis.

You have been put on this earth to fulfill something greater than what you might once have believed. Creating your Sacred Agreement is one way to enhance your personal growth and raise your potential to a higher level of consciousness. It also becomes a consistent reminder that choice is your greatest power and that you hold that power within you every moment of every day of your life. When you are faced with hard decisions, your Sacred Agreement can pull you back to your divine potential—it is a symbolic reminder of the strength, power, and enormous capacity that lies within you. Your Sacred Agreement is also a personal message center that shouts, "Hey, look alive!" "Stand up for yourself!" "Make the most of who you are and what you know you can become!" "Never stop trying!"

> At the site of the ancient Oracle of Delhi in Greece, inscribed above the entrance are the words "Know Thyself."

I don't believe that a book like this ever really finishes. It just stops in interesting places, and that's when you, the reader, take over, massaging the material and information and adapting it to meet your own specific needs and future plans. One way of reminding yourself to do this is by crafting a Sacred Agreement. Let the following template be your guide, but don't let it prevent you from using your creativity to make your Sacred Agreement more meaningful for you. It can be whatever you choose. To refresh your memory on the specifics of what each commitment entails, refer back to the introduction to this book.

My Sacred Agreement

So that I may further live my life in ways that make the best use of my authentic self, my strongest competencies, my greatest gifts, and my higher purpose in life, I commit myself to the following three directives on my soul map as I continue my journey to True North:

I Will Pay Close Attention to and Honor My Inner Guidance System, Making My Personal Growth and Self-Development a Top Priority

List the ways in which you have committed to doing this:

_____

_____

_____

What are the time frames you have set for yourself?

_____

_____

Describe the ways in which you will push aside your fears and self-doubts on your journey to True North:

_____

_____

I Will Use My Intellect and My Faith in Tandem

How will you maintain faith in yourself?

_____

_____

How will you maintain faith in something greater than yourself?

_____

_____

_____

How are you flexible? What priorities and goals are you going to readjust?

_____

_____

_____

How are you both smart and faithful at the same time?

_____

_____

_____

I Will Focus on the Present and Start Living Forward. My Mantra Is "No Martyrs; No Victims."

How are you aware of every moment that is happening to you, right here, right now?

_____

_____

_____

How and when did you get off the road in the past? What did you experience as a result?

_____

_____

_____

Describe how you are living your life forward.

_____

_____

_____

What is your vision for a better tomorrow? What is your greatest hope?

_____

_____

_____

I joyfully make the above commitments in this Soul Agreement and will review, update, and renew my commitments on the following date: _____

_____

Signature   Date

The purpose of creating a Sacred Agreement with yourself is to remind you of the importance of continuing the process of inner renewal, self-development, and lifelong learning. The frequency with which you revisit your Sacred Agreement is up to you. Some people revisit their Sacred Agreement every month; others do so only once a year.

Let this agreement help you to solidify your overall relationship with your authentic self and your authentic power.

Embracing True North—The Most Comfortable Direction You Have Ever Felt

I believe that when you embrace True North, you embrace the good life. In their book *Repacking Your Bags: Lighten Your Load for the Rest of Your Life* Richard J. Leider and David A. Shapiro offer one of the best formulas for mastering the good life that I have ever read: "Living in the Place you belong, with the people you Love, doing the Right Work, on Purpose." I couldn't agree more.

For me, Leider and Shapiro's formula for the good life poses four poignant and relevant questions that we all need to take a look at.

> "A contract isn't about saying what you meant. It is about meaning what you say."—OLIVER WENDELL HOLMES, PHYSICIAN, POET, AND HUMORIST

1. Are you living in the place where you belong?
2. Are you with the people you love?
3. Are you doing the right work?
4. Are you living your purpose?

My recommendation is that at some point you sit down and take the necessary time to contemplate the profoundness of these questions that can be gleaned from Leider and Shapiro's book. Answer them honestly and allow your inner guidance system to move you forward.

My Wish for You

It is my hope that in the pages of this book you have found a source of inner peace and greater passion, patience and expectation, love for yourself and love for others. Remember, whatever *was* is in the past, and tomorrow is *yet to be* realized. The one true

> "The important thing is this: To be able at any moment to sacrifice what we are for what we could become." —CHARLES DU BOIS

thing is this very moment, right here, right now—the only moment in time that you have for certain. What will you do with it? I hope you will cast your eyes to the north sky and keep moving in your quest to discover your True North. Here is an important question that I am often asked in workshops and that you may be asking yourself right now: "How will I know that I am on the path to discovering my True North?" I tell people, "You will know, because it will be the most *comfortable* direction you have ever felt." Here is where I leave you to explore, shape, and define your life's purpose, potential, and passion. Set your sights on your own North Star, keep your life compasses and navigation tools at hand, and follow the destiny that you and you alone will choose to create.

And one last note: The journey is the destination.

Bibliography

This bibliography lists materials that I have referred to, that have inspired my work, or that have helped to shape some of my ideas over the years in preparation for writing this book. It is not meant to be a complete record of all the works and resources I have consulted throughout my years of writing, training, and public speaking. Rather, it is meant to express the range and substance of the research that I have conducted that I feel is in some way relevant to this book.

PREFACE

Bolen, Jean Shinoda. *The Tao of Psychology.* San Francisco: Harper & Row, 1979.
Cameron, Julia. *The Artist's Way.* New York: Tarcher/Putnam, 1992.
Dalai Lama. *The Art of Living.* New York and London: Thorson/HarperCollins, 2001.
Moore, Thomas. *Care of the Soul.* New York: HarperCollins, 1992.
Williamson, Marianne. *The Healing of America.* New York: Simon & Schuster, 1997.
Zander, Rosamund Stone, and Benjamin Zander. *The Art of Possibility: Transforming Professional and Personal Life.* Boston: Harvard Business Press, 2000.

INTRODUCTION

Adrienne, Carol. *The Purpose of Your Life.* New York: Eagle Book/William Morrow, 1998.
Arrien, Angeles. *The Four-Fold Way.* New York: HarperCollins, 1993.
Beck, Martha. *Finding Your Own North Star.* New York: Crown, 2001
Geldard, Richard. *The Spiritual Teachings of Ralph Waldo Emerson.* Great Barrington, Mass.: Lindisfarne Books, 2001.
Keyes, Ken. *Handbook for Higher Consciousness.* Coos Bay, Ore.: Love Line Books, 1975.
Millman, Dan. *The Life You Were Born to Live: A Guide to Finding Your Life Purpose.* Novato, Calif.: New World Library, 1993.

CHAPTER 1

Alessandra, Tony, and Michael J. O'Connor. *The Platinum Rule: Do unto Others as They'd Like Done unto Them.* New York: Warner Books, 1996.
Anderson, Walter. *The Confidence Course.* New York: HarperCollins, 1997.
Bruce, Anne. *Building a High Morale Workplace.* New York: McGraw-Hill, 2003.
Ford, Debbie. *The Dark Side of the Light Chasers.* New York: Riverhead Books, 1998.
McGraw, Phillip C. *Life Strategies: Doing What Works, Doing What Matters.* New York: Hyperion, 1999.
Wickman, Floyd, and Terry Sjodin. *Mentoring: The Most Obvious yet Overlooked Key to Achieving More in Life than You Ever Dreamed Possible.* Chicago: Irwin Professional Publishing, 1997.
Woititz, Janet. *Home Away from Home: The Art of Self-Sabotage.* Pompano Beach, Fla.: HCI, 1987.

CHAPTER 2

Bennett-Goleman, Tara. *Emotional Alchemy.* New York: Harmony Books, 2001.
Buckingham, Marcus, and Curt Coffman. *First Break All the Rules.* New York: Simon & Schuster, 1999.
Cameron, Julia. *God Is No Laughing Matter.* New York: Tarcher/Putnam, 2000.
Freiberg, Kevin, and Jackie Freiberg. *Nuts! Southwest Airlines' Crazy Recipe for Business and Personal Success.* Austin, Tex.: Bard Press, 1996.
King, Stephen. *On Writing—A Memoir of the Craft.* New York: Scribner's, 2000.
Reichheld, Frederick F. *The Loyalty Effect: The Hidden Force behind Growth, Profits, and Lasting Value.* Boston: Harvard Business School Press, 1996.

CHAPTER 3

Buzan, Tony. *The Power of Spiritual Intelligence: 10 Ways to Tap into Your Spiritual Genius.* New York: HarperCollins, 2001.
Cooper, Robert K., and Ayman Sawaf. *Executive EQ.* New York: Grosset/Putnam, 1997.
Ford, Debbie. *The Dark Side of the Light Chasers.* New York: Riverhead Books, 1998.
Goleman, Daniel. *Working with Emotional Intelligence.* New York: Bantam Books, 1998.
McGraw, Phillip C. *Self Matters: Creating Your Life from the Inside Out.* New York: Simon & Schuster, 2001.
Reynolds, David K. *A Handbook for Constructive Living.* Honolulu: University of Hawaii Press, 2002.
Richardson, Cheryl. *Stand Up for Your Life.* New York: The Free Press, 2002.

CHAPTER 4

Bloch, Douglas. *Listening to Your Voice Within.* Center City, Minn.: Hazelden Foundation, 1991.
Cameron, Julia. *Heart Steps.* New York: Tarcher/Putnam, 1997.
Fortang, Laura Berman. *Living Your Best Life.* New York: Penguin Putnam, 2001.
Frank, Anne. *Anne Frank—The Diary of a Young Girl.* New York: Penguin Books, 2001.
Giuliani, Rudolph. *Leadership.* New York: Hyperion, 2002.
Jeffers, Susan. *Feel the Fear and Do It Anyway.* New York: Fawcett Columbine, 1987.
Jenkins, Roy. *Winston Churchill.* New York: Farrar, Straus & Giroux, 2001.
Millman, Dan. *Living on Purpose.* Novato, Calif.: New World Library, 2000.
Morrissey, Mary Manin. *Building Your Field of Dreams.* New York: Bantam Books, 1997.

CHAPTER 5

Bolles, Richard Nelson. *What Color Is Your Parachute 2003.* Berkeley, Calif.: Ten Speed Press, 2002.
Bruce, Anne. *Leaders—Start to Finish.* Alexandria, Va.: ASTD Publishing, 2001.
Chang, Richard. *The Passion Plan at Work.* San Francisco: Jossey-Bass, 2001.
Collins, Jim. *Good to Great: Why Some Companies Make the Leap . . . and Others Don't.* New York: HarperCollins, 2001.
Goleman, Daniel. *Emotional Intelligence.* New York: Bantam Books, 1997.
Leider, Richard J. *The Power of Purpose.* San Francisco: Berrett-Koehler, 1997.
———, and David A. Shapiro. *Whistle While You Work.* San Francisco: Berrett-Koehler, 2001.
Lorsch, Jay W., and Thomas J. Tierney. *Aligning the Stars: How to Succeed When Professionals Drive Results.* Boston: Harvard Business School Press, 2002.
Palmer, Parker. *Let Your Life Speak.* San Francisco: Jossey-Bass, 2000.
Rothwell, William J., and Henry J. Sredl. *The ASTD Reference Guide to Professional Human Resources Development Roles and Competencies,* 2d ed. Amherst, Mass.: HRD Press, 1992.
Shriver, Maria. *Ten Things I Wish I'd Known before I Went Out into the Real World.* New York: Warner Books, 2000.

CHAPTER 6

Cameron, Julia. *Walking in This World.* New York: Random House, 2002.
———. *The Artist's Way.* New York: Tarcher/Putnam, 1992.
Eckhart, Tolle. *The Power of NOW.* Novato, Calif.: New World Library, 1999.
———. *Practicing the Power of NOW.* Novato, Calif.: New World Library, 2001.
Frost, Nina H., Kenneth C. Ruge, and Richard W. Shoup. *Soul Mapping.* New York: Marlowe & Company, 2000.
Helliwell, Tanis. *Take Your Soul to Work.* Holbrook, Mass.: Adams Media Corporation, 1999.
Loehr, Jim, and Tony Schwartz. *The Power of Full Engagement.* New York: Free Press, 2003.
Shaughnessy, Susan. *Walking on Alligators.* New York: HarperCollins, 1993.

CHAPTER 7

Altea, Rosemary. *You Own the Power.* New York: Eagle Brook/William Morrow, 2000.
Artress, Lauren. *Walking a Sacred Path.* New York: Riverhead Books, 1995.
Einstein, Albert. *Ideas and Opinions.* New York: Modern Library, 1994.
Einstein, Patricia. *Intuition: The Path to Inner Wisdom.* Boston: Element Books, 1997.
Gawain, Shakti. *Developing Intuition: Practical Guidance for Daily Life.* Novato, Calif.: New World Library, 2000.
Helliwell, Tanis. *Take Your Soul to Work.* Holbrook, Mass.: Adams Media Corporation, 1999.
Soul Stories. New York: Simon & Schuster: 2000.

CHAPTER 8

Bruce, Anne. *Building a High Morale Workplace.* New York: McGraw-Hill, 2003.
———, and James S. Pepitone. *Motivating Employees.* New York: McGraw-Hill, 1999.
Gafni, Marc. *Soul Prints.* New York: Pocket Books, 2001.
Helliwell, Tanis. *Take Your Soul to Work.* Holbrook, Mass.: Adams Media Corporation, 1999.
Zoglio, Suzanne Willis. *Create a Life that Tickles Your Soul.* Doylestown, Pa.: Tower Hill Press, 1999.
Zukav, Gary. *The Seat of the Soul.* New York: Fireside/Simon & Schuster, 1990.
——— and Linda Francis. *The Heart of the Soul.* New York: Simon & Schuster, 2001.

CHAPTER 9

Ban Breathnach, Sarah. *Romancing the Ordinary.* New York: The Simple Abundance Press/Scribner's, 2002.
———. *Simple Abundance.* New York: Warner Books, 1995.
Bellman, Geoffrey M. *Your Signature Path.* San Francisco: Berrett-Koehler, 1996.
Bluestein, Jane, Judy Lawrence, and S. J. Sanchez. *Daily Riches: A Journal of Gratitude and Awareness.* Deerfield Beach, Fla.: HCI, 1998.
Bryan, Mark, with Julia Cameron and Catherine Allen. *The Artist's Way at Work: Riding the Dragon.* New York: Quill/William Morrow, 1999.
Chopra, Deepak. *The Seven Spiritual Laws of Success.* Novato, Calif.: New World Library, 1994.
Eldon, Kathy, and Amy Eldon. *Soul Catcher.* San Francisco: Chronicle Books, 1999.
Goldberg, Natalie, and Judith Guest. *Writing Down the Bones.* Boston: Shambhala Publications, 1986.
Kushner, Harold S. *Living a Life That Matters.* New York: Knopf, 2001.
Lewin, Roger, and Birute Regine. *The Soul at Work.* New York: Simon & Schuster, 2000.
Myss, Caroline. *Sacred Contracts.* New York: Harmony Books, 2001.
Ryan, M. J. *Attitudes of Gratitude.* York Beach, Me.: Conari Press, 2001.

CHAPTER 10

Carter-Scott, Cherie. *If Life Is a Game, These Are the Rules.* New York: Broadway Books, 1998.

Pierce, Linda Breen. *Choosing Simplicity: Real People Finding Peace and Fulfillment in a Complex World.* Carmel, Calif.: Gallagher Press, 2000.

Quindlen, Anna. *A Short Guide to a Happy Life.* New York: Random House, 2000.

St. James, Elaine. *Inner Simplicity: 100 Ways to Regain Peace and Nourish Your Soul.* New York: Hyperion, 1995.

Thorpe, Scott. *How to Think like Einstein.* Naperville, Ill.: Sourcebooks, Inc., 2000.

Trout, Jack, with Steve Rivkin. *The Power of Simplicity.* New York: McGraw-Hill, 1999.

CONCLUSION

Aftel, Mandy. *The Story of Your Life—Becoming the Author of Your Experience.* New York: Simon & Schuster, 1996.

Cameron, Julia. *Walking in This World.* New York: Random House, 2002.

Ford, Debbie. *The Secret of the Shadow.* San Francisco: HarperCollins, 2002.

Jones, Laurie Beth. *The Power of Positive Prophecy: Finding the Hidden Potential in Everyday Life.* New York: Hyperion, 1999.

Leider, Richard J., and David A. Shapiro. *Repacking Your Bags: Lighten Your Load for the Rest of Your Life.* San Francisco: Berrett-Koehler, 2002.

Maxwell, John C. *Becoming a Person of Influence: How to Positively Impact the Lives of Others.* Nashville, Tenn.: Thomas Nelson Publishers, 1997.

GENERAL

Branden, Nathaniel. *The Power of Self-Esteem.* New York: Barnes & Noble/HCI, 1992.

Calaprice, Alice. *The Expanded Quotable Einstein.* Princeton, N.J.: Princeton University Press, 2000.

Dalai Lama. *Ethics for the New Millennium.* New York: Riverhead Books, 1999.

Gray, John. *How to Get What You Want and Want What You Have.* New York: HarperCollins, 1999.

Helliwell, Tanis. *Decoding Destiny.* Toronto, Canada: T. A. Helliwell Publications, 1988.

Keith, Kent. *Anyway.* New York: Putnam, 2001.

Nowinski, Joseph. *6 Questions that Can Change Your Life.* Emmaus, Pa.: Rodale, 2002.

Peck, Scott M. *The Road Less Traveled.* New York: Simon & Schuster, 1978.

———. *The Road Less Traveled and Beyond.* New York: Simon & Schuster, 1997.

Peters, Tom. *The Circle of Innovation.* New York: Knopf, 1997.

Richardson, Cheryl. *Life Makeovers.* New York: Broadway Books, 2000.

Ruiz, Don Miguel. *The Four Agreements.* San Rafael, Calif.: Amber-Allen Publishing, 1997.

Seligman, Martin. *Authentic Happiness.* New York: The Free Press, 2002.

Senge, Peter M. *The Fifth Discipline.* New York: Currency, 1990.

Williamson, Marianne. *Everyday Grace.* New York: Riverhead Books, 2002.

Zukav, Gary. *The Dancing Wu Li Masters.* New York: Morrow Quill, 1979.

Index

About the Author

Over the years, Anne Bruce has evolved from the best-selling author of several books in the field of human behavior, leadership, and motivation to an inspirational force and a respected specialist, speaker, and trainer in the area of human development and personal growth. Thousands of people around the world have adopted Anne's no-nonsense approach to Discovering True North and have learned to be the "authors of their life stories." Anne's workshops and keynote presentations, including this book, grew out of her powerful and life-changing courses taught worldwide, known as the *Human Potential Series: Inspirational Programs with Substance and Soul.*

Anne Bruce passionately demonstrates, with nuts-and-bolts transformation tools and techniques, the steps necessary to build on our signature strengths and to rely on the magnificent inner guidance system that is within us all.

Anne's books, such as *Building a High Morale Workplace* (McGraw-Hill, 2003), *How to Motivate Every Employee* (McGraw-Hill Professional Education, 2003), *Leaders—Start to Finish: A Road Map for Developing and Training Leaders at All Levels* (ASTD Publishing, 2000), and *Motivating Employees* (McGraw-Hill, 1999), have inspired thousands of people and have been translated into more than a dozen languages worldwide.

A former television talk show host and producer for CBS, Anne has been a featured presenter for the White House, Harvard and Stanford law schools, and the London Institute of Management. Her motivational programs on leadership, customer service, the power of human potential, and an array of communications topics have been featured at worldwide business conferences, at professional associations, and in hundreds of corporations, including Coca-Cola, Sprint, Ben & Jerry's, Southwest Airlines, The Southern Company, Lanier Worldwide, Blue Cross/Blue Shield, Paine Webber, Baylor University Medical Center, the American Red Cross, and the Conference Board of Europe.

Anne has appeared on the *CBS Evening News with Dan Rather, 48 Hours, Good Morning America,* MSNBC, and the *Charlie Rose Show.* She also has been interviewed for a number of stories in the *Wall Street Journal, USA Today,* the *Times* (London), the *Boston Globe, Newsweek,* and the *San Francisco Chronicle.*

For more information on workshops, retreats, and keynote presentations associ-
ated with this book, visit Anne's web site at www.annebruce.com to get a workshop
outline and details on how you can bring this program into your organization. Or
you can e-mail questions and comments to anne@annebruce.com. Anne resides in
Charleston, South Carolina, with her husband, David, and remains profoundly
enthusiastic on her continuing journey to True North. She can be reached by calling
214-507-8242.